The Wilderness Rape

a story

The Wilderness Rape

a story

Jack Wayne Chappell

THE NEW WEST HOUSE

THE WILDERNESS RAPE

ISBN 0-9614974-0-8

Library of Congress Catalog Number 85-061472

Manufactured by Publisher's Press, Salt Lake City, Utah.

PRINTED IN THE UNITED STATES OF AMERICA

COVER PHOTO: Little Camas Prarie by JERRY KENKE of Nature's Way Photography. To order 11 x 14 prints from the gallery of one of Idaho's finest photographers, send $35 to Nature's Way, 390 N. 9th East, Mountain Home, Idaho, 83647.

To order collector's copies of the forthcoming novel entitled *ANGELS DON'T SLEEP*, send $14.95 to THE NEW WEST HOUSE, Box 175 Bruneau, Idaho, 83604. These books will be hardbound, 6 x 9. Price includes tax and postage. To order softcover copies of THE WILDERNESS RAPE, from the same address, send $5.95 per copy, price includes tax and postage.

LITERATURE!

FROM THE NEW WEST HOUSE

PREFACE

Someone once said that a good book needs no preface.What the statesman failed to acknowledge is that a preface is, in truth, an afterward.

Writing is an art form. A writer is an artist. What he portrays is sometimes done in a fervor, and there is not always time, beforehand, to consider the objective. Therefore, an afterward becomes a prerequisite.

Justice is swift for the writer. He never determines the literary value of his product.That decision is left, so viscerally, to the audience. It is this allocation of value that should preside over his every chain of thought.

He must, when taking a stand, remove himself like a sly priest, from all radical dogma, and from all bigotted assumptions. Yet, there is no infallible writer, in this fact rest assured.

You can have the most sophisticated, Ph.D'ed, documented, bibliographied, indexed book in the world—and the audience may refuse it even an audition.

THE WILDERNESS RAPE has had its audition. It is the people of the Western States that have born it's completion, and if the Wilderness issue had been properly resolved, this manifesto mightn't have had an audience.

The success of this story was determined by people who bought orders on a prepaid basis, many of whom did not receive their books as promptly as they should have (putting it mildly).

The book suffered atrocious setbacks. The first fifteen thousand were published and delivered on time. The next ten thousand were contracted to a printer that took bankruptcy and defaulted on the deal. New orders had to be taken to offset the loss, and rebuilding the program took manifold more effort than the publisher had ever imagined. But, in the end, perseverance paid, as it always does, when an idea is on solid ground.

But, if it had not been for the support, patience, and fortitude of the people whose lives and heritage depend on proper management of public lands, this message would not have flourished.

To these people, who paid and waited, I need to express my warmest, deepest thanks. Success is assured. The extent of our impact is the only determination that floats on the wing.

We can come together on the Wilderness dilemma—not in the form of any more "compromise", but rather, in a final agreement.

In reality we are again faced with an allocation of value. It has been determined that existing designated Wilderness areas have more value as such that they would if managed under multiple-use proviso. It is as simple, and at once as complex as any other allocation of value.

It is simple stuff. Vital stuff. Like a pristine stand of North Idaho cedar at the five-thousand foot level, and a grey forest of bug-killed lodgepole at the four thousand foot level. When lightening strikes the grey forest in the dead of August, and the grey forest goes up in smoke, you can kiss the resources that

2

could have been harvested *and the pristine forest* good-bye. Simple stuff like that.

It is as simple as a band of backpackers who lament and wail about the abuses of public lands by ignorant visitors, and "environmental" groups who spend millions lobbying in favor of the lock up of public lands by the federal government, when if they had spent a fraction of their time and money organizing cleanup clubs and reclamation programs, the problems would have been solved before they began. Simple stuff like that. The kind of stuff that equates to *really caring*.

The fear is that the cybernetic world will gobble up the remnants of the natural world, and obviously, the fear is justified. But the solution is highly objectionable. The solution that the "environmental" groups propose is the carte blanche takeover of public lands by federal authoritarians, and the transfer of private lands into the hands of the federal bureaucracies. The solutions that these "environmental" groups have proposed, and are proposing, is failure. Failure to communicate, failure to agree, failure to respect the lives and liberties of the inhabitants of the Western States, and failure to separate the fallacies from the realities.

It is not the trademark of a highly evolved society that they should be at each other's throats in a desperate struggle for existential needs, and it is not a feather in the cap of the oncoming generation that they become expert at control through coercion and propaganda.

If this simple story does not give you other areas of thought to roam—ares outside of the Wilderness issue—then it will not have been for lack of intent.

As I close this preface, which is really an afterthought, I want to tip my hat to you, the reader, and offer my appreciation for your patronage.

May we all live, love, and prosper.

****

3

THE EDITORS at the New West House would like to take this opportunity to introduce two more of Chappell's works that are nearing publication.

The first is entitled *THE BRIDLEMAN*, and it is an enchanting story of a Western life, with the violent reality of sudden death; the miracle and the iron passion that love fuses together, composed of the higher quality of literature that audiences of this age are seeking out.

The author began work on this classic tale with pen and ink, under the light from a Coleman lantern in the winter of 1972. He completed the first six hundred page draft sixteen years later in the spring of 1988.

Critics have called it "a monumental portrayal of a way of life that most people don't even know exists."

Exciting, powerful, masterfully written, and of timeless value, this novel will take its audience to a world of beauty, danger, romance, and reality.

THE BRIDLEMAN is not an escape, it is an explosive adventure, from the pen of a master of the art.

The second novel, entitled *ANGELS DON'T SLEEP*, is a lovable, hateable, odyssey—an excursion into a philosophical wonderland that few writers would have dared to dwell in. The original printing will be collector's copies, signed by the author, and available by special order only. Standard trade hardcovers will be available in bookstores late in 1989.

Join the introverted, extraverted, psyched-up and spaced out villainous hero in a journey that gallops through the galaxies of the human mind, then be ready to plant your feet on solid ground. This novel is a grand exploration of the world's

4

most tangled emotional and intellectual traps and escapes, written with a simplicity that hooks you from the first page, leads you through a land of romantic wilderness heretofore untrod, and always, *always,* entertains.

ANGELS DON'T SLEEP breaks all the rules, and smashes the worn out standards of mediocrity in today's publishing industry by daring to tell the untellable story of a heretic's search for an eternal love.

This is publishing the way it was meant to be. Bold. Naked. Unafraid. There has never been a book like this one before, and may never be again. It is total, uninhibited, freedom of expression, and at The New West House, that is our goal.

For those who wish to order collector's copies in advance, we have provided an address on the copyright page of this manifesto. The originals will be numbered and signed in the order that they are sold.

All the personnel at our New West House, including the printers at Publisher's Press, wish to provide you with the highest quality of literature, at the most reasonable price. It has been intimated that today's publishing industry is abandoning the art. Here, we put it on a pedestal. If you appreciate what we have tried to do for you, the customer, then please compliment our effort by encouraging your children to master the art of experiencing fine literature. Literature without a well educated audience is not literature at all, for the art is only in the mind of its audience.

To master any art, we must first learn to serve the art, and with us, serving the art is more than a grand intention, it is an uncompromised promise.

THE EDITORS

THE WILDERNESS RAPE

a story

Sheets of dust in an evening storm moved like eerie shadows, casting a glowing red aura over the eternal desert. The splendid glow of the crimson sun was drowned in a sea of sand; not a howling, raging wind, but a quick, strong shift of sky. Horses on a distant slope abandoned their feed to run for the shelter of the creek bank, manes and tails flying.

A spray of thick, brown raindrops go before the storm and pelt against the wall of an old log cabin in the valley of the long grass, then the valley is engulfed by the aura, and the raindrops die. Winds whisper like spirits of ancient times as the sand sifts along the grooves between the logs of the cabin; a pulsating rain of powdered earth drifts against the window pane; willows by the stream bow low in the waning light, and fade into oblivion.

In the cabin, the light is a flow of golden rays that cannot cut the solitude. The fireplace murmurs back at the wind with its wavering flames and dull red glowing coals.

The sheepskin rug before the fireplace affords a soft retreat for the pensive young woman who stretches herself, catlike, before the fire. There is an almost inaudible hum from the recorder as the long playing reels trace the sounds inside the room. When she speaks, the machine listens.

"Can anyone foresee a time in the future when the entire society will be made up of young, strong, physically fit beings who cannot relate to the natural world unless it is inaccessible to those less fortunate?

6

"Will there be no older folks, or toddlers, or physically or mentally impaired? Will there be no need to utilize resources available and vital to regional economies? Will there be no reason to guide these souls, and will they live by instinct in the shelter of their caves? Some souls would prefer the cave to the home, I suppose, and fires sparked from flint to heat from a power plant. And some would believe that the spirit of a naturalist is more valuable than the spirit of a natural man."

She shed her clothing, for the fire was warm, and the sheepskin against her body was a precious luxury. Bourbon on ice made it perfect for her—she was alone in the wilderness—she feared no one—she needed no one. The bourbon warmed her inside as the fire without.

"I want to tell you some stories," she said, "and I hope that you can make the pieces fit together by the time my presentation is concluded....

"I don't want to bore you with heavy rhetoric and tedious inquisition. I just want to keep you awake throughout my dissertation, and I hope to bait you somewhat, with my stories. They are my testimony to a way of life that I can't forsake, and hope to leave as my legacy.

"Bear with me through stories that you don't immediately correlate. My stories are all tied to a specific point in this protest. I want to tell you real life stories, but I also need to lay a foundation for a structure that can only be built in the heart. This is one environmentalist's manifesto in protest of legislation that has been sponsored by people who claim to be environmentalists themselves.

"I want to tell you a story about wild horses," she said, and she drew back the bolt to a door in her mind that held adventures untold. "Wild horses....and a man named John....

"John and Pete were Oregon buckaroos; ragged, rowdy, and always hunting sport. I rode with them one spring on a trip I made through southeastern Oregon, and it was one of the happiest times that I can recall.

7

"We were moving cattle to the mountains for the summer, and as we gathered the Catlow basin, we were always on the lookout for wild horses to run.

"A twenty-mile-long rim rose on the eastern border of the valley, and breaks came down the rim from the mesa high above. Though the rim was sheer, it ran a shifting, broken line, and wherever a break came down, many game trails cut through and stretched to the valley floor. Deer, antelope, and mustangs that wintered on top of the mesa liked to come down the breaks to feed on the early growth of forbs and cheat grass on the slope below the rim.

"If it happened that a couple of buckaroos could cut off a little bunch of mustangs by blocking their flight back up the break, then they'd be hemmed under the sheer rimrock, and, not knowing the way the land lay in the valley, they'd be easy picking. Of course, we looked sharp for this type of deal, and one morning as we set out for our day's ride, we ran into it.

"When we saw the wild horses on the slope below the Dry Creek Draw, nobody said a word. Old man Miller's thoroughbred stud had sired wild horses in this country, and some of them made good saddle horses. This bunch we knew, and the big brown stud was sure a decent type, not inbred at all. His colts were what we wanted, for the young ones would tame right down. We had the jump on this bunch, and we all hit a high lope, making to cut them off from the draw, for if they made the top, they'd be on a rocky flat where we wouldn't have a chance at catching them. They spotted us then, and they bolted for the draw.

"John was up on Easter, his favorite outside horse, one that had been a wild horse as well when he was a colt. They left Pete and I behind as they whipped up the trail to cut the mustangs back into the rimrock. Being behind, we fell past the drag of the mustangs, and blocked two game trails that went out over the breaks in the rim. We'd all had our pick of that bunch of horses, and a two-year-old pinto looked like the best one.

"John got his job done, and when the mustangs turned, we had them cold. With all trails blocked, they took down the draw, and John disappeared in a stand of juniper trees, as Pete and I fell in ahead of the mustangs to head them off again. A twenty foot cutbank kept them from crossing the dry creekbed, and it ran for a quarter of a mile, forcing the mustangs right at Pete and me. The brown stud had his lead mare flat out in front, but she smelled out the trap, and broke back too soon.

"We could have lassed the brown stallion right then, as he stalled, trying to fight the lead mare back, but we knew he'd be rank, and would never be trustworthy. We wanted young stuff to trade off as saddle horses, and not the broomtailed types, either; we wanted the fleet-hoofed pinto with the streak of thoroughbred in him from his ranch-raised grandsire.

"They all turned, then split up and took through the rocks, making toward the mesa, trails or no trails. It was all Pete and I could do to haze the pinto back against the cutbank. He panicked, and turned up the trail. We scrambled like hellions to beat him back the other way, and when he turned again, he had us beat, and he knew it. He stretched out down that dry creek bank, sailing like a leaf in a gale.

"Pete and I were out of the race, but John, crafty as a cougar, had spurred his horse through the junipers, and into the creekbed. With Easter scattering sand in the air behind them, they tore down the draw.

"Totally unaware of the danger directly below him, the pinto mustang was running neck and neck on the creek bank twenty feet above. When a wide trail came up out of the sandy bottom, Easter bounded to the top, and a rawhide lass-rope whirled in the air.

"The pinto saw the trap, and he veered fast away, but the loop sailed out, and the slack sang tight. Dust ripped up from the ground in puffs where the pinto struck as he pitched into the sky, and back to the ground. His jaws flew open, and he let out a scream! With ears pinned flat back, with his long mane flying, he was lassed at the end of a rawhide reata, and his front feet flailed out, punching holes in the Oregon wind!

****

9

"The adventure in the breaks of the Oregon wilderness is a treasure that can never be stolen. I'll have that moment until I die, and maybe longer—no man can take it from me.

"But what we did back then is a serious crime today. Today, if we were caught running wild horses, we would be fined and imprisoned. We would be evil, you see, for our cruelty to animals, and we would be displayed in the papers as criminals against society. Criminals and outcasts, locked away behind a concrete wall.

"We would be labelled *'heartless cowboys who can't care about animals unless they can be ridden on top of, put on as attire, or eaten for dinner.'* Were that the case, I suppose you could call us *'criminally insane.'*

****

"The misinformation that goes out makes the Western people ruthless exploiters with no conscience and no remorse. Ruiners of ranges, and levellers of forests.

"Yet, considering that our livelihoods depend on the quality and volume of our resources, why would we want to *'exploit'* the resources that our future depends on? Wise resource management and conservation are the Westerner's chief concerns. Our lives depend on conservation of natural resources, a fact of which we have been aware for generations, and there are none more competent, or more capable of preserving the Western way of life than the people who make the West their home.

"If you'll read a few books, you'll discover that some of the world's most learned scientists, economists, and sociologists have urged a regionally based government.

"I stress the injustice of centralized authority, and submit that citizens of states, regions, and communities have a priority right to preside over and manage resources on public lands, even though those resources may be the property of the nation collectively, and I base this belief on the premise that residents of a region are more acutely aware of the specific problems that crop up in those regions.

"Westerners are Americans too, you know, with rights no lesser than Easterners, and metropolitans.

"The problem is, for every congressman we have in Washington D.C., there's twenty-five of the sons-of-guns from the metropolitan areas!

"As long as the eco-freaks and environmental zanies can keep deluding the masses into believing that the way to *'save Bambi'* is to lock up all the public lands, we don't stand a snowball's chance in hell. We are so badly outgunned, that we don't even have a vote. In Idaho, we have two congressmen—in the whole state! And 85% of our state is either owned or controlled by the federal government!

"Now, I want you to take just a moment to think about this, before I go on with my stories. In isolated western regions, up to 98% of the land may be owned by the fed. All of our resources come off those public lands. If we don't have access to our resources, we're broke—we're bust—no joke!

"In America (which is supposed to be a capitalistic nation) 33% of the continental land is already owned by the bureaucracies! There is not one, single, solitary elected representative in the Bureau of Land Management, or the U.S. Forest Service, and they have absolute power over regions that make up over a third of the country!

"You can't imagine the incredible amount of waste that goes on. Karl Marx would eat his heart out trying to compete with the onslaught of American socialism that we're seeing out here today.

"So to leave this part, and pick it up later, I will pause with a little story.

"A logger in Northern California was walking home in the dusk, in August of 1988. A gunman stepped up behind him and put a pistol to his ear. 'Who do you want for President', the gunman demanded, 'Bush, or Dukakis?'

"The logger pondered. 'Quick,' said the gunman, 'make up your mind before I blow your brains out!'

"The logger pondered for just a moment longer, and then he replied, 'Well, when I get to thinking about it, it doesn't really matter—you might as well go ahead and shoot!'

"Now, of course, this story was just for fun, but I'm going to tell you some stories that are for real, so stay with me....

"While eighty percent of the people live on two percent of the land, the Western heritage is being ground into powder by folks who are really quite sincere in their belief that they are serving a worthy cause. The city people are not trying to wipe us out intentionally, they just don't know any better. They aren't even aware that we have a problem—and if we do—well, then, that's our problem, not theirs—right?

"Just because they have us out voted by about a jillion to one, and just because we have no power within our states to hold the federal government at bay, why should it be of any concern to the people in New York and L.A.?

"Well, it might be a good idea to inform them that they are losing their possessory interest in public lands right along with the rest of us.

****

"I'll bet that no one can calculate the sum of the incredible waste that has gone on out here. I'll bet the billions of dollars that were squandered will never be totalled. I'll try to quote you a few small examples as I go along.

"Now, some of my stories are for fun, and some of them are for fact. This one is for real.

"North of Dubois, Wyoming, in the Bridger-Teton National Forest, there was a hundred million board feet of timber that just *blew down*. Because it was in a designated Wilderness area, *they wouldn't even let the loggers save the deadfall!*

"They made them leave it there, and let it rot. Now, the Forest Service had already cut back their resource base to the point that timber harvest was no longer possible, so the mill shut down. Let me tell you friend, when a mill goes down in one of these little western towns, the whole damn town goes with it. Our forest resources are left to rot and burn.

****

"Let us observe the wicked, evil, California logger. See him cut down the redwoods. He is evil, yes he is! You can just see it in the grim, hard lines of his face, the callouses on his hands, and the way he strides among the pines as though he owns them, choosing which he will destroy. My God! The evidence is overwhelming! Look! Look! Look at him cut down the trees! He cuts down trees to make money, because he's greedy, and wants to feed his family. He wants to raise sons to cut down more and more trees! Soon there will be no trees! Are you blind? Can't you see it? He is so despicably evil, *can't you see?*"

She caught her breath.

"Let me explain some things so that you can understand," she went on, "why those rugged loggers might not be such horrible people after all." She thought for a moment.

"I don't have a degree in forestry. That's a fact. I don't have a degree in anything except common sense. When it comes to that, most of us can qualify. But let me toss out a few mountain girl ideas, so you can weigh some of the real evidence for yourself....

"First, if you get a true old growth forest, you can't have a second growth. Duff builds up under the old trees, and the seeds can't penetrate. The seeds (and sprouts) have to have mineral soils, air, sunlight, and water, before they can grow. Old forests defeat all these ingredients, and there is no room for young timber to come up. At this point there are two ways to make room for a new growth of forest:

A. Cut down the old growth and use it for lumber, or:

B. Wait for mother nature to erase the entire forest by fire.

"Either way, the area comes back with browse (brush), grasses, broad leaf species, and new growth forest. "Our most treasured big game species thrive on a balanced diet of many plants, including a large quantity of browse, broadleaf plant, and grass, but browse and broadleaf in particular. To the best of my knowledge, the best conifer in the big game species' diet is provided by young timber.

"Loggers create millions of tons of forage for big game animals by harvesting old growth forests. If they don't do it, mother nature will. This is not for maybe, it's a simple fact.

"The natives and informed newcomers out here know that we're losing hundreds of thousands of acres of mature timber stands to fires and insect infestations. Note the historic fires in dead forest areas after the trees had fallen prey to pine beetles and spruce budworms. At this time, the rampant fires that cleaned out the thousands of infected acres of timber in the Yellowstone National Park are still smoldering.

Dateline, San Francisco News:

Tourists in Yellowstone marvel at spectacular forest fire, wonder of nature!

"Well, in a national park, I suppose it's futile to argue with the fed. But the bugs came into that region from the east side, and had already wiped out thousands of acres of public lands in and east of Island Park, and we're losing hundreds of thousands of acres in areas that are supposed to be managed under multiple use guidelines. That particular blanket of bugs (that set the stage for the Yellowstone fire of '88) started in Idaho, and spread into many parts of Montana, and Wyoming. If they think the Yellowstone fire was peachy keen, I'm sure they'll all smile real pretty when another fire takes out a hundred mile radius all around the park....come to think of it, that would be a good excuse for them to proclaim the whole area a *new wilderness!*

"It's common knowledge out here that some trees are diseased, or infested with parasites, and should be harvested before the fires take hold and rage out of control, demolishing not only the grey forests, but spreading to healthy forests as well. Other trees must be left to seed offspring, and provide conifer for our ecosystems. We've learned it from our fathers, and we'll teach it to our children, who will love this country with the same passion that we have ourselves. Our grandparents knew it, and our grandchildren will too.

"How many city people, though, even understand that when an area is *designated Wilderness* by congress, it locks up our entire resource base, and leaves those millions of acres to be devoured by insects, and wiped out by fire? When the mills are shut down, and the loggers are out of work, and our timber base is *'preserved in its natural state,'* how many metropolitans are even vaguely aware of the disastrous consequences that surely will follow?

"Do they know that all our existing roads are closed, that all the best hunting and fishing accesses are denied, that when they come to our west, they'll soon discover that what used to be public domain wherein every citizen of America had a possessory interest will be locked up tight for the exclusive use of a select few?

"Do they know that areas where my father used to take me when I was a little girl have been shut down, and rendered so inaccessible that my own toddlers are expected to hike for scores of miles just to get to the Saturday morning fishing hole?

"SAVE THE WILDERNESS!!!

The cry goes out to metro America.

The last of the Wilderness will be devastated if it isn't preserved!!

"Why should it be so difficult to make people understand that nearly a hundred million acres have already been locked up into designated Wilderness, with brutal disregard for the rights of private citizens, and the environmental zanies have plans to lock up a hundred and fifty million more?

"Why should it be so tuff to go eye-to-eye with the metro audiences and explain that the millions of acres locked up into 'designated' areas doesn't even include the National Parks, Wild and Scenic Rivers, State Parks, game Refuges, Bird Refuges, and special use areas?

"Why should it be impossible to get the message out to the downtown crowds? Why would they think that a log cabin and a logging road are wicked, and that massive burn outs are acceptable?

"How could any American, supposedly raised with faith in the values of human equality, ever be led to believe that a few million lives out west are perfectly expendable in consideration of the lofty ideals promulgated by the Wilderness Cults that drive us from our very homes?

"And who can deny that the dogmas hoisted into stately grandeur by the 'environmental' leagues are anything other than that? And don't blame me for coining the phrase 'wilderness cults'—it was coined by Roderick Nash in his analytic book, *Wilderness and the American Mind.*

"I read the thing, and was appalled at the way Mr. Nash dispensed with us as degenerates who have inherited an innate bias against the wilderness from primate ancestors who were unable to survive in the forests. According to his theory, we are all prejudiced against the wilderness—we hate it—that's why we want to tear it down.

"The irony never ceases to amaze me. All the priests of the wilderness cults are city people who live in a world of concrete and glass. They come out West and see a clear cut where a forest used to be, and wailing like banshees, wend their tearful way to Washington D.C. with the sad tidings of the *devastation of the wilderness.'*

"They never take time to casually observe that if our forest and range resources were left unharvested, that those lovely millions of acres would be rotting with age and going up in smoke.

"Sure, different regions are confronted with different evolutionary cycles. It doesn't take a brainchild to figure that out. In the Pacific Northwest, for example, we have hundreds of thousands of acres of bug-killed timber, but out on the California coast where the redwoods grow, the bug problem is practically non-existent. (The redwoods are highly resistant to insects.)

"But answer me this: Why should it be that the people in New York and L.A. have more control over the management of public lands in Idaho than the Idahoans do? It's the same story in ten other western states. In Alaska they locked up thirty five million acres, and they want thirty million more! Wyoming, California, Utah, Colorado, Arizona, Nevada, Montana, Oregon, and a big chunk of New Mexico—we're all in the same boat, and it's sinking! Why should it be that democracy is surrendered to mob rule?

"In spring of 1988, a judge in the ninth circuit court in San Francisco locked up the entire Yak River drainage in Northern Montana when an environmental cult lawyer waxed eloquent about the danger of exploiting habitat for the great Grizzly Bear.

"Apparently, nobody told the judge that grizzly bears don't eat trees. In fact, the people of Montana didn't even know that the case was going to court. The result was the shut down of the entire region. It put the loggers out of work, took the lion's share of the money right out of the region's pocket, and worst of all, left the spread of tree-killing insects unchecked.

"In reality, the loggers were in no way harmful to the habitat of Mr. Bear. Quite the contrary, as a matter of fact, but since there are twenty million people in southern California, and less than a million in Montana, and since the land does belong to the fed, ignorance, arrogance, and mob rule prevailed.

"Again, you don't have to be an Einstein to figure out that grizzly bears do not eat bug killed timber. You don't have to be possessed with an amazing brain to understand that an aged forest, harvested, will return a young, healthy, vigorous forest where old Mr. Bear will be much better off.

"Unfortunately, the case wasn't decided in the best interest of the ecology. It was decided in consideration of the emotional whim that has been so popular in southern California, and the people of Montana could go politely to hell if they didn't like it.

"Do you think that the logger is evil for what he does? Or do you even think about it at all? Think about it the next time you estimate the cost of the construction of a new home, or when you watch film footage on national television of forest fires that wipe out our inland west.

"I heard a logger talking the other day. Do you know what he said? He said:

'The minute you lock up a wilderness area, you have no more constitutional rights. You go in as the guest of the government, under their rules. You take it off the tax roles; it is no longer self-supporting in any way. It not only becomes an economic burden to the people, it gives the bureaucrats absolute control. Our schools are underfunded, are economies are drying up, and when the country goes up in smoke, the eco-freaks just sit back chanting, *burn, baby, burn! Ain't it natural! Just the way God would have wanted it!*'

"Strange we should lay the blame for our western disasters and wrecked economy on anyone else's doorstep. The fault is our own. It is the citizenry that has allowed the lock up of all our wilderness lands to go on without a worthy battle. When urban nerves are an edge over foreign wars and pestilences, it's almost a bright spot to see our federal legislators up to something as seemingly harmless as locking the public off the public domain.

"It is the citizenry that has allowed the substitution of counter-productive 'doublethink' logic for reason and good judgement. It is out of ignorance that we accept the lies that are imposed upon us, and out of cowardice that we cleave to legislated conformity instead of holding on to our personal identity. It is apathy that leads us to forsake our natural morality, and forsaken morality that bids us submit to the anonymous authority of irrational law.

"When an isolated individual strikes out against society, we try him and punish him. But, when our society strikes out

19

against the isolated individual, doesn't our crime go unpunished?

"When we cower behind the banner of nationalism, and let irrational authority run rampant, do we believe that our victims are guilty for the simple reason that they did not conform to the whim of our mystical dictum?

"Tell us to walk, we walk. Tell us to lie down, so do we. Tell us to be silent, we will. Tell us to commit social suicide, package it prettily, and watch us cut our own throats. We will. We have no choice, for we are afraid, and it is the monster we have created that we fear. We fear there is no escape, and so our guts wrench in violent throes, but we follow sickly down the primrose path.

"Soon we shall have a judgement, and we shall imprison a victim of our own cowardice—a victim of irrational law. We will put our victim away, and disguise our ugliness in blind, angry, dogmatic enthusiasm for a prettily packaged fraud. Then we will gloat—until we discover our folly—we will have imprisoned our children—and our children's children."

****

"I'm going to tell you something special," she said, and she moved to the hearth.

"As I said, I'm an environmentalist too, like most any real Westerner is. In truth, anybody who loves the natural world and tries to do right by it will qualify for that title. If I love the natural world, care enough to do my best to keep the garden green, why shouldn't that make me a part of it? I think it does, in more ways than one. Out here, our spirits revolve around the outdoor life. The way we're brought up, it becomes a part of us, body, mind, and soul.

"When I was young, I had a best friend named Gale. Gale was an Idaho boy, straight as a lodgepole pine. We rode our ponies on the upland deserts among the ranchers cattle, and over eternal ranges. We fished and hunted in the mountains, ragged kids from Idaho, free as the air! Where Gale went, so did I, and where I went, so did he. We grew up the way our grandfathers did—in the Idaho wilds.

"How many trails we travelled, I don't know—I couldn't count them all. Two barefoot pals pounding our tracks in the dust among the pines, and wading in the creeks with our pants rolled up, catching rockrollers to use for bait and hook the native trout on our homespun rods. And how many kids out here grew up that way? So many...Oh! So many!

"Then one day, an accident took Gale to a higher plane of existence. My lifelong friend was gone. Everyone who knew him mourned and went on with their lives, but I couldn't go on with mine. A young adult, I was confused, and lost, so lost!

"I drove up into the Trinity Mountains in the Sawtooth Range of central Idaho, and I stayed there for a couple of weeks.

21

No one came around. I cooked my meals over my fire, and spent some time hiking around. I caught a few trout from an unnamed creek, and sat up night after night, gazing into my fire and listening to the wind, talking to the pines.

"Then I found him. It was the wind in the treetops without touching the ground that told me the answer to my sorrow. He was there! I heard him laughing from the waterfall, and whistling from the willows! I saw him bouncing down the trails in the shadows of the pines, and scampering over the rocky cliffs and ledges, just the way he used to do so long ago when we were as wild as the trails we travelled.

"Gale was there! His spirit was part of it, like mine, and like my grandfather's. Gale was alive, as he is right now, and he laughs beside me on the same unnamed trails whenever I go back to the Trinities.

"He talks to me in a more perfect way, and I love him in a more perfect way—whenever I go back there.

"I ask you, now, do you think that I am wicked to want to take my children back to the places where Gale and I learned to love the wilderness, just because I want to drive there, as I have done all my life? Would it be so selfish to ask that our little road to the Trinities be left open for generations to come?

"And if I return to discover that a logger has cut down a section of my beloved forest, do you think I can't understand the cycles of life and death in the forest? Gale and I knew from the time we were small that old forests die and rot. Those old trees will not give ground to the new ones unless there is a harvest. And why not let a logger make an honest living for himself and his family? Why not let him raise up a little barefoot boy, just like Gale, who will grow tall and strong like the young pine trees in the Idaho wilds......

"And so, my memories are yours," she said, and she spent a thoughtful moment in mental recluse. "There are many memories...." her voice trailed off, then reflectively began again.

****

22

"Oh, but you're missing the point!" wail the eco-cults. "*In the wilderness, man must be a visitor who does not remain!*"

"Too bad they forgot to tell the public we been living out here for several generations. Oh, well, the public didn't think about that.

"Perhaps I should throw in a small anecdote, just to lighten things up a little." She stretched herself, unwinding a bit. "I'll tell you a story about a hardpan knoll in the Utah desert.

"There was a hardpan knoll that had collected a cover of sand. As it aged, pioneer grasses covered up the sand, and built humus. Perennial grasses took over the humus soil for many years until a plague of Mormon crickets reduced it to ground level two years running.

"The next year was very dry, and when lightening struck the hardpan knoll, the perennial grass burnt out before it could refurbish itself, and a three-day wind blew ashes and sand over onto an adjoining ridge. A few stems of rabbit brush came up on the knoll, and these, along with a weak sprinkling of pioneer grasses, held on to the sparse covering of the hardpan knoll. After a few years, the humus built up, and the plants began to prosper once again. Seeds of gramma grass came in on the wind, and soon there was a stand.

"Buffalo came along, and drove the gramma grass out. Annuals took over once more, and a few perennials, like sage, and rye grass came up.

"Then one day, a cowboy came by, driving a small bunch of cattle. Seeing a black storm brewing on the skyline, he herded his cattle into a brush patch beside the hardpan knoll. When the storm came in, it was hailstones the size of golf balls, pounding the struggling soils on the hardpan knoll for over an hour.

"When the storm went away, the hardpan knoll was a pulverized shambles, and the soils went washing off the knoll to the toe of the slope, where they lodged, creating a long, deep bed of organic matter and sand.

"The cowboy mused at the hardpan knoll, and went his way. The next spring he returned with a load of salt on his pack horse, and to his surprise, a wild-eyed environmentalist was conducting a tour of the hardpan knoll. There was a botanist from Lansing, a paleontologist from Boston, and a writer from New York.

'What we have here,' said the botanist, *'is the literal evidence of the devastating effect of overgrazing on the environment.'* *'This is what we call desert pavement,'* said the paleontologist. *'You can see that the damage was recently inflicted. A classic case of overgrazing, followed by a severe rainstorm. Nature will need a century of preservation to repair this unholy mess!'*

'I reckon it's a hardpan knoll, not pavement,' thought the cowboy, *'and it weren't overgrazed, and it weren't a rainstorm. It were a hailstorm, and I seen it, fer I was hunkered under my saddle blankets, only twenty feet away.'*

"But the botanist was talking about the lecture he was planning for the esoteric club in Lansing, the paleontologist was talking about his doctorate degree, and the writer was taking pictures of the hardpan knoll for the paper in New York.

"So the cowboy kept his peace, and when they were gone, he set his salt blocks out on top of the hardpan knoll.

"Every deer, every cow, every antelope, desert bighorn, and wild horse in the area began to laze for salt on top of the hardpan knoll, and soon there built up a considerable layer of manure. When the salt blocks were gone, the cowboy put out new ones, on a different section of the knoll. Soon the knoll had collected many, many feces, and the cowboy changed his salt ground.

"The next year, a crop of hardy pioneer grasses covered the hardpan knoll from one end to the other, and humus was rapidly collecting. When the cowboy rode by, he smiled as he looked at the country, and admired the view. Along the trail home, he happened again onto the botanist, the paleontologist, and the writer. They were talking about the devastating effect of dirt biking on the fragile desert floor. The scientists were making calculations and talking about their federal grant for studies. The writer was taking pictures as fast as she could snap them.

"As the cowboy unsaddled his horse that evening, he thought about his experience, and spoke to the animal.

'*You know, Old Red,*' he said to his horse, '*you buy them books and you send them to school, and what the hell do they do? They eat the covers.*'

"Now of course, this anecdote was a product of my imagination," she smiled as she lazed on the rug, "and I don't mean to try and tell you if anything of this nature has ever actually happened. But the next time you hear some city-bred environmentalist raving about the devastation of the ranges, perhaps you should take it with a grain of salt."

****

"How many thousands of articles in metropolitan magazines and newspapers have ranted and raved about the destruction of western forests and rangelands? And how many of the writers have had the slightest idea what in the world they were talking about?

"How many odious ramblings were written about desertification, deforestation, and outrageous abuses of public lands?

"How many national commercials on TV were put over by celebrities like *Hollywood Clint and Hollywood Charles ?*

'Get the bad guys off public lands!' Hollywood Charles sells his revere so solemn and splendorous.

'They can clean up their act, or get out of town!' Hollywood Clint dashes his steely gaze into the minds of the overwhelming millions.

"And the uninformed millions who watch these celebrated antics have no idea what devastating consequences their nationalistic efforts will reap, and no suspicion that ulterior motives may be involved.

"Unfortunately, the *bad guys* include all the poor souls who make the West their home, and even though that insinuation is never clearly stated in the commercials themselves, it sure as hell comes across that way.

"What it tells the general public is that anybody who cuts down a tree is a bad guy. Anybody who rides a dirt bike is a bad guy. Anybody who depends on a natural resource to provide their family with a livelihood, *these are the bad guys!*

"And, naturally, anybody who sends money to help wipe out the *bad guys,* well, then the *good guys* who want the socialist left to run rampant over one third of the entire continent, they'll certainly appreciate the money, and the federal bureaucracies, they'll wax powerful strong, filled with unbridled authority. Then, anybody who dares to call this cult-styled philosophy exactly what it is will be promptly labelled a *right wing industrialist.*

"Let me give you an example of the kind of treachery that the *'environmental good guys'* are up to.

"The sainted *good guys* are into tree sitting and tree spiking, in their blessed effort to save our forests, so that mother nature can come along later and burn them down. The objective is to drive us out of business, and let nature take her course.

"In a New York Times bestseller, *Hollywood Richard, the celebrated author, went into a lengthy discourse on his effort to save the forest. 'We'll spike your trees!'* He raves. Then he talks about how much he cares for Bambi.

"So the *good guys* will spike our trees in sanctimonious piety!

"On May 8, 1987, at a mill in Cloverdale, California, a headrig hit an 11" spike in a log, and virtually exploded. A piece of the saw hit mill employee George Alexander in the head. Although he was wearing a safety helmet with a face shield, the saw cut through his left cheek, jawbone, tore out his teeth, and cut two jugular veins. Alexander was taken by ambulance to a local hospital and was later transferred to the University of

California Medical center in San Francisco. He's lucky to be alive, but will bear the scars of the incident for the rest of his life.

"Now don't misunderstand, I don't blame Hollywood Richard for putting his anger into words. He's a great writer, I'm bound to confess, and I love his books, when he sticks to the things he knows about. I don't think he had any idea that tree spiking is violence without cause. He simply seemed to have no real concept of the nature of our environment, and was looking at it from a very uneducated perspective. Somebody bullshitted him into believing that tree spiking is *the* thing to do, that's all. If he'd spent a few years among the loggers, he might have known better than to think that way.

"But of course, this tree-spiking tactic is applauded by our enviro-cult friends, and has been openly advocated throughout the entire United States.

"Disregard the fact that an unharvested forest goes to ashes. Spike the trees, by all means! And get national celebrities to stand up and cheer!

"What in God's name motivates these people? I can answer that question for you in one word:

DOGMA!

****

"I want to tell you another story about horses," she rejoined, "horses, and another man, this one named Jim.

"Jim loved horses. He hadn't spent years with horses, but he'd read a lot of cowboy stories, and he'd seen a lot of western movies where the magnificent wild stallion rears into air.

"And, he'd been horseback riding on at least several dozen occasions.

"Now, old Jim, he bought a colt from me one time, and wanted his new colt penned in a small corral. This colt was not your ordinary backyard horse. He was a range bred three-year-old that had run free in the Southern Idaho wilderness all his life. He was neither halter broke, nor broke to ride. Jim couldn't get the horse into the pen.

"Jim isn't just your ordinary man, either. He's a man who proclaims his love for the wilderness, and all the wild creatures of the world.

"Now that's just fine with me. I have no argument with that. I love the wilderness, and the wild creatures myself. But at least I've been blessed with some intimate contact with the country and the wildlife. But Jim? He couldn't even pen his new colt! Around the pen it raced, dodging the gate, and getting past him at every turn. His timidity and lack of experience told the horse all it needed to know. Any old country girl could have penned the colt in a matter of seconds, but not Jim. Finally, he turned to me for help.

"I asked him to get out of the corral so that he'd not be in the way, then I took up a hank of rope and whirled it, turning the horse back twice against the corral fence. After that, I sent the colt toward the pen, intimidating it with the hank of rope.

Jim was astounded when the horse trotted into the pen, and I swung the gate closed.

'I've been here for nearly an hour,' he said sheepishly, and you did that in ten seconds.'

"I said nothing, but thought to myself that this is a man who has had so little experience in the wilderness that he can't even pen a colt. He knows nothing of the balance of ecology on our ranges, yet he joins the cults to lead the charge for the lock up of our lands. He knows nothing of the cycles of weather, grass, insects, and animals; he can neither read sign, or even survive out of his element any longer than a week long backpacking trip. This is a man who testified in favor of the wild horse protection act that put hundreds of honest ranchers out of business, and wiped out our ecosystems. He testifies for wilderness legislation at every hearing he can attend, and now here he is, displaying his helplessness in my corral. This man, whom I have just helped to pen a colt, is a fellow who claims expertise in environmental matters, who damns the Westerner as a ruthless exploiter of the land, and wants the federal bureaucracy to strip me of my way of life. Here he is, pretending to be my friend, when in reality, his dogmas are a threat to my heritage, and my way of life.

"He got his education in a classroom full of city kids, just like himself, and his mind is full of distorted impressions about the wilderness that he took from the environmental *good guys* who have plundered us for so long. This man, who can't even pen a colt, thinks himself to be a wiser manager of wild lands than a woman like me who spend her entire life out here!

"A blank look crossed Jim's face when he read the obvious anger in my eyes. He had done nothing he could think of to distress me, and was taken back when my obvious ire left me silent. He couldn't know what was going through my mind. He thought it brutally unfair that I was angry for no apparent reason. It was all I could do to keep from despising him at that moment. A wild rage ran through me. Were men like him my enemies? The *do good by force and by fraud* ethic that motivated people like him made me think of a finger on the trigger of a gun. *'Is the government's gun pointed at my head by brainwashed men like this?'* I thought.

"That's the reason for this recording. It is the only rational means for me. It is the only weapon I have. But let me go on, and tell you more about Jim and his horses.

"So Jim loved horses, especially wild ones. He'd never seen a wild horse, but he loved them anyway. He loved them so much, he thought, that by God, it was his duty to protect them. He took action on that account many years ago....let's go back a few years.....

"Over a decade ago, little children in their classrooms on the east coast were enticed by their teachers to write letters to their congressmen, and the response was overwhelming. Included in their little notes were hand fashioned crayon and pencil drawings of little wild horsies. The title of their effort was:

PLEASE SAVE MY PONY!

The result of this heartstopping entreaty (and the barrage of propaganda from the metro USA that went along with it) was:

The Wild Horse and Burro Protection Act.

"If the crayon and pencil drawings had been of feral dogs and cats, what would have been the inevitable result? *The Stray Dog Protection Act?*

"But nonetheless, we were the *bad guys*, and we were all condemned in pious indignation. The wicked ranchers were the obvious villains, and the wild horse enthusiasts were the obvious heroes.

"Now, over ten years later, after metropolitan ignorance of the subject matter prevailed, and was fully exploited, take a look at the clandestine results.

"Huge reserves were set aside, and the overpopulations of wild horses are now costing the taxpayers from twenty to fifty million dollars per year. Oh, it's a very nebulous figure, all right, and the bureaucracies just love it that way!

"But at least the city folks saved the endangered species, right?

"Wrong. The mustangs were never endangered to begin with, they were never a species to begin with, and there was a constant flow of wild horses in and out of all the herds, which kept the ecology in balance.

"You disagree? You heard about all the federal money that was doled out to enterprising university and government biologists, nature study programs, wildlife organizations, and pandering socialist professors who proved conclusively that these wild horses are really *Barb Mustangs*, a unique and endangered species? You even watched them on national TV?

"Hey, that's pretty neat," she grinned, almost laughing at the gullibility of the public at large. "I watched it on TV, too! An experienced eye could *actually read the brands* on the so called 'wild mustangs' that were galloping splendidly across the screen on the nightly national news!

"And do you know why they call them the *Barb Mustangs?* Well, because many horses were imported by the Spaniards from the Barbary Coast. It is presumed that they selected the horses for size, regardless of age or gene traits, because of the size of the compartments on the boats, and there was no genetic selection involved at all. The claim that the Barbary horses were gene specific is just as ludicrous as the claim that any feral horse is gene specific. The best bred Spanish horses were derived from expensive bloodlines *all over the world,* and the American wild mustangs were mutants from every breed of horse under the sun, not only from Barbarian descendants, but from every pilgrim who ever brought a horse to stateside, and turned it loose on the range.

"Throughout the Western States, the only true breed of early American range horses were those developed by the Nez Perce Indians through selective breeding. They call them *Appaloosas.* The rest, and all the rest, *were feral horses with gene frequencies from all over the globe!*

"But the sanctimonious left had a great talent for spreading the gospel of the American Mustang, symbol of freedom and liberty.

"Now, over a decade later, our dear bureaucracies are spending millions of our tax dollars to fly them in with helicopters, castrate the stallions, spay the mares, adopt them out to private citizens, and stick them in elaborate feedlots ten thousand head at a time, feeding them dairy hay at a hundred dollars per ton that the dairy farmers can barely afford. There's your symbol of freedom and liberty, corralled, castrated, and locked up in a feedlot. Go look at it, if you don't believe me! "And did they stop the incidences of cruelty to the poor wild ponies? Let me toss you a news bulletin, and this is a true story:

"*Dateline, Reno, Nevada. BLM assumes blame for roundup that led to the deaths of forty-eight wild horses that were driven unmercifully in hot weather! University of Minnesota researchers had plenty of money to study the situation. They had attached radios to twenty-eight animals, and implanted tracking devises in sixteen mares. Reports indicated that the horses were released in an area that kept them from migrating north to familiar ranges. They walked a drift fence for miles in both directions until they finally, slowly, died an excruciating death from dehydration.*

"Sorry gang, but that's a true story. There's what happens when you send in the federal incompetents to manage your natural resources. There's an example of how our federally funded wild animal lovers have proven to us beyond question that we didn't know what we were talking about when we tried to tell them that the mustang was never endangered, and was never a unique species........But wait! There's more!

"Perhaps the rural Americans should come down on the city dwellers for the cruel and sadistic murder of thousands of innocent dogs and cats by horrible and torturous means. Perhaps we should hold a rally on the White House lawn to lobby for *The Stray Dog Protection Act!* We could get millions untold from the fed to study the impact of feral cats and dogs on the metropolitan ecosystems! The dog is a great symbol of man's concomitance with nature, and his most trusted and allied servant! The common alley cat is a throwback from the wild cats of prehistory! And you talk about endangered! Dog catchers should be cast into prison! How can they possibly feel justified in snatching the last of the wild animals in metro-America, to torture and execute them thereafter?!

"So, I trust that any urban citizen can understand why stray dogs must be adopted or destroyed. Why, then, was it totally impossible to educate people to understand that wild and free roaming horses and burros were no more endangered as a species than are wild and free roaming dogs and cats? Could it be because they were all hoodwinked by the tons of propaganda that poured out from their little square TV boxes on the nightly news, and all the grandiose literature that was published against the wicked ranchers who were such obvious villains and liars? Could it be that all our pandering professors were selling us a bill of goods?

"Or do the wild horse enthusiasts still swear that they were in the right?

"Well, the numbers of western mustangs were not going to dwindle as long as ranchers had grazing permits for certain numbers of horses. You see, as the range horses matured, small groups of young studs and fillies broke away from the main bands, to form their own groups. This was caused by the natural pecking order in the herds. The dominant studs would drive off the young studs, and these, in turn, would go wild, and steal mares from other bands.

"It was worse than absurd to claim that the ranchers wanted to wipe out the wild horse populations, (although a few of them would have, had it been feasible to do so) because the ranchers were the ones who perpetuated it in the first place! And ya know what happened? The B.L.M. revoked all the grazing permits for range horses!

"The protest went up under the glare of emotional hysteria that was spread in the papers and on TV.

WILD MUSTANGS WERE BEING CAPTURED AND SOLD FOR
SLAUGHTER!!!

"So the city people changed all that in one hell of a hurry. Today, the same people spend somewhere between twenty and fifty million dollars per year (the bureaucracies and pony panderers are very discreet about the release of actual totals) to put our dear ponies through the most outrageous cruelty that the wildlifers ever devised. After tortuous chase scenes with helicopters, steel chutes for castration, spaying, and implantation, locking them up by the literal tens of thousands in the most expensive feedlots ever devised by man, the eventual result will be that these feral critters will end up in the stomachs of French Poodles in New York anyway!

"Before, a handful of mustangers could make a few extra bucks, and keep the eco-systems balanced.

"Now, the taxpayers are spending millions, wiping out private rangelands, driving innocent people out of business, overgrazing to the point that other game must move out, and the cruelty to the feral horses is appalling.

"But, since the good folks in suburbia don't know the difference, their emotions are placated. The blatant ecological disaster that followed the Wild Horse Protection Act was totally predictable, and it sure keeps the wild pony panderers a lot quieter than they used to be. Don't worry—everything is under control. You bet! Do the bureaucrats love it? Well, the benefits are handsome.

"And what can the Westerners do about it today? Well, just sit back, pour a glass of wine, and say, *'We told you so, but you wouldn't listen.'*

"Endangered species—the feral horse? It doesn't take a brainchild to discover that wild horse populations were not endangered. But then there was the aggrandized claim to deal with, you know the one—mustangs were a specific breed, totally unique from all other species of horses, and in need of protection if only for that sake.

"Well, that was bullshit, too. We all knew it.

"Now, I am not a professor of equine phylogeny, that's true, but I do lay claim to a certain amount of common sense.

"I can see that when a particular group of birds all bear the same prominent characteristics, they can be classified as a unique species. The male Mallard, for example, has a green head, the female a brown head, and they do not vary except in the case of a hybrid, such as a Mallard crossed with a Pintail, in which case the hybrid is not a member of the Mallard or Pintail breed, neither is it a breed of its own. In the case where a hybrid is potent, it may cross back, or outcross, but one gene will normally dominate, pulling the gene frequency back to the mainstream.

"In dogs, there are specific breeds; all of these sharing common traits. Color traits, structural traits, traits of habit (as in birdhunters), and traits of character (such as gentleness, protectiveness, viciousness). Therefore, it is easy to see how one particular model can represent a certain breed.

"But what is there in the mustang that is common to a particular breed?

"Wildness? Hell, any horse turned lose on the range as a colt and allowed to run free will become wild and unmanageable. Many backyard horses, raised domestically, may become wild and unmanageable due to poor handling. I therefore discount wildness as a genetic trait, on the grounds that any breed of horse can become wild and unmanageable as easily as any bird of the wing can fly.

"Structure? The only similarity in the structure of mustangs could be listed as:

"1. Smallness, due mostly to inbreeding and malnutrition. If fed from the weanling stage, a mustang will grow as large as its particular phenotype will allow. For instance, if it is the descendant of a rancher's good thoroughbred stud, it may grow quite tall. If it is the victim of inbreeding, it may remain quite small.

"2. Large, unsightly heads, and pan feet. This is not common to all mustangs, only the inbred and inferior. Although inbreeding can produce desirable characteristics when directed by human management, the effect for practically all mustangs is a dulled mind, and a marred form.

"3. Long, matted manes and tails. Of course any ungroomed horse will grow a long mane and matted tail.

"4. Habits? Their habits conform with any other breed of horse left to adapt to the wild environment. When captured, some will become gentle, others not, according to their individual genetic background, and also in accordance with good or bad handling. (Phenotype = genotype, plus the effect of the environment.)

"I find not one thing indicating that the mustang is a specific breed, different from all others, except that they are wild and free roaming. In this respect they are no different than a wild and free roaming dog.

"Many is the time I've seen the pony lovers on TV pointing out *'Barb characteristics'* to a totally ignorant metro audience. The dished face, the width between the eyes, the bullshit goes on interminably. These characteristics can be found in individual breeds of horses all over the world. The pony panderers want to keep their federal porkbellies, even if they have to lie and plunder to accomplish that end.

"And by the way, they have the votes, we don't. Even though there has never been any valid evidence to support the idiotic theory, the tons of garbage heaped upon the urban mind passed for evidence, and when you're talking about the federal dole, that's close enough. The idea that wild horses are, were, or ever have been in danger of dwindling is worse than propaganda.

"The actual truth is that before the wild horse act was passed, the mustang populations were well balanced, and the market for feral horses was free.

"Today the results are ridiculously obvious. It should go down as one of America's most ludicrous fiascoes, but trying to take away those millions from our pony-faced friends is like trying to take religion away from the Ayatollah. No malice intended. I think of it as a challenge to set it back to the way it used to be, and to use it to point out the future failures of the bureaucracies that will surely follow, if the fed is allowed to continue with its authoritarian control of public lands.

"Give the mustangs all the protection you want, just turn the managerial responsibilities over to the individual states, let public lands officials be elected to their positions, and get the federation the hell out of it entirely, that's what I think. Me, and ten million other citizens of the inland west.

"It is a desecration to the ideal of self government when a handful of radicals can undermine an entire social class, their heritage and lifestyle, through centralized bureaucratic government, and political subterfuge.

"And if you have gobbled up the propaganda on the mustang fiasco, I shan't apologize for enlightening you."

She shut off the recorder and lounged for a while, quite at home with her message. the firelight danced on the ivory swell of her breasts, and the rug sighed against the silky nakedness of her legs. Presently she took up her mission at the recorder.

"Even though the facts assured that if wild horse protection were legislated, the *ecosystems*, the *big game* and *other wild animals*, the *ranchers*, *sportsmen*, the *regional economies* and the *mustangs themselves* would all suffer, the legislation *passed* through the spirited efforts of people who swore they knew what they were talking about!

"Do the same hysterical radicals still refuse to allow the repeal of their folly? And does the propaganda go on? How could they have been wrong? And by virtue of the merit of the plea *Save My Pony*, wasn't the whole urban world led astray?

"The western mustang, in limited numbers, scattered seed through its feces, utilized range inaccessible to other grazing animals, packed the bottoms in waterholes tight, and kept the trails open.

"In large numbers, its double row of long, strong teeth and rock-hard solid hooves destroy perennial plants, doing damage in a decade that nature will need the help of human reclamation to repair.

"Worse by far are the wild burros. Take their malicious nature into consideration, along with the fact that in our desert ecosystems, we have a very limited supply of water. If you have fifteen bands of burros in a region with only a half-dozen waterholes, there is going to be one band of burros at every waterhole every day. The burros will fight all other types of wildlife, big game animals in particular, away from waterholes and salt grounds, driving them completely out of the region! It's a simple fact. If deer, bighorns, antelope and cattle can't get to the waterholes, they can't use the region! We tried to tell them that before the measure passed, but would they listen? Hell no. Not with all that federal money at stake. So the taxpayers in the cities got what they deserved, but what about the ecology of the range? And what about private rights on public lands?

"So what are the pony people going to do now? Well, naturally, they want to condemn private property on a massive scale to make more room for more wild ponies. They want to revoke more grazing rights from the cattlemen, drive as many as they can out of business, and set up more playgrounds for our pandering professors, and federally funded students of natural resources. (Educate these youngsters so they can get a good job in the bureau.)

"It shouldn't take too much arm twisting to accomplish this feat. I mean after all, they have the zeal of the god-almighty masses on their side.

"When you wake up in the morning and wonder whatever happened to one third of the continent, when you simultaneously discover that it doesn't end there, that the bureaucracies are condemning private property rights across the board, and are already so powerful that they can hold the western states hostage at will, then maybe you'll think twice about the difference between the socialistic system, and the free enterprise system.

"The greatest treachery of all is the stripping of the individual's rights through centralized authoritarian control. The Westerner can throw an absolute fit in his outrage, as long as he keeps it at home. That's about as far as it will go. The state has no say-so in the matter, because public lands are the property of the fed.

"Likewise with the wilderness legislation. It's all railroaded through congress based on emotional whim, preordained, and pompously solicited by the far left friends.

"These groups, like one major mountain club whose name I need not even mention, really don't give a damn how many Westerners are stripped of their heritage and their way of life, or how many families are plummeted into poverty by the theft of vital resources on which their livelihoods depend.

Jim, the man who loved horses, was convinced that the mustang bill had been passed in the best interest of the nation. I told him that there was a big difference between nationalism and patriotism. Patriotism is allegiance to your country in terms of it's moral and ethical values, which must constantly be questioned, tested, and proven. Nationalism is blind allegiance to the authority of the fed, whether it's right or whether it's wrong. Patriotism is a virtue. Nationalism is a disease.

"It seems that our bountiful homeland has been targeted for a Marxist's playground, and the western way of life is being kicked aside as so much dung beneath the feet of these *looters* who aggrandize themselves as *'friends of the environment.'*

"Once, a few adventurous cowboys had balanced the mustang numbers to the environmental conditions, and had done so as an integral part of the ecosystems. *The mustang was about as 'endangered' as the common coyote.* So why did the bureaucrats jump into bed with the radicals? I'll have to leave that question to your fifty million dollar imagination.

"And closing here, I wish for you to note the correlation between the mustang bill and the wilderness bill. The methods of packaging, of marketing, and the social aspects of the product in the two bills are practically identical.

****

"Clear cut timber and open pit mines that scar the land, chemical dumps and nuclear power plants have outraged the conscientious, and embittered the masses, who utilize them on the one hand, and despise them on the other.

"Demagogues emerge, pitting the emotions of the one faction against the emotions of the other. We see the naturalist squared off against the industrialist.

"Soon a beautiful piece of emotional, irrational legislation becomes a new law, to placate the spirits of the masses, and convince the demagogues that their crusade was with just cause.".

She laughed then, it was so absurd.

"Has it ever been you fortune to behold a curious phenomenon from occasion to occasion in your dealings with others—the strange longing to continue to live with multiple petty lies even though the truth has become self evident?

"Have you ever wondered at the way certain individuals seem overwhelmingly content in their submission to these vain pretenses, or the way they react with such malice toward any and all who threaten to penetrate their armor with the sword of truth?

"When the pretenders have so deceived themselves, brainwashed themselves, that they deny the very existence of any evidence supportive of a contrary claim, and when the truth threatens their dogmas with change, their cause immediately takes on the characteristics of martyrdom. The lies are perceived to be truths—the truth is perceived as a wicked, insidious threat to their ostentatious banner, hence to themselves, as they are at one with their purpose.

"But no matter how vainly the pretenders cling to their illusions, the end result is always that their world comes crashing down around them, leaving them tearful, in some cases repentant, but usually vengeful. The magnetic strength of irrationality, especially collective irrationality, makes one wonder if it has any other purpose than to speed the destruction of human existence.

"By studying the dogmas that our wilderness cults thrive on, any halfway intelligent human will soon discover that the destruction of human existence has become the cultster's consummate goal. Humans, (especially the wicked ones who believe in being free) are viewed with contempt, and the anti-man philosophy becomes so obvious, it's amazing that the media won't touch it. Makes a girl wonder if the press hasn't been bought off.

"Just dare to insinuate that the environmental cults are backed and orchestrated by American leaders of the socialist left, and you've got yourself a throng of cults hooting:

Bambi Killer! Tree Murderer! Mountain raper! The last of the redwoods are being executed in Humboldt County, California! The last of the wilderness is being annihilated by strip mining in Nevada! Our wildlife species are becoming extinct! Our world is being devastated by greedy capitalists! We must call upon the federal government to save us from this monstrous evil! The time to act is now! Our national treasure is at stake! Please, teachers, you can help! Get the children to believe us! Teach it in our colleges and universities! Get the political guns aligned, and blast these wicked land abusers off the face of the earth, else your children will never see the glory of the wild!

"And the good old boy who has to work ten hours a day, seven days a week to support all the pandering professors, welfare environmentalists, fat bellied bureaucrats, and crooked politicians, he's expected to pay all the bills without using a plow or a chain saw. Well, like I said, Karl Marx would eat his heart out trying to compete with what America has grown at home. You gotta hand it to us. When we do it in America, it's whole hog or none.

"Let me toss in a few examples of the way a myth takes hold, and refuses to die. Let's just start with a couple of obvious examples, for the sake of expedience. I think that by the time we've run through a couple more, you might begin to believe that what I told you about the mustang myth is damn sure the truth. Let's tackle this one first:

The last of the redwoods are being viciously executed in Northern California!!

"The fact is the that from over one hundred million years ago, these trees were extant in many parts of the world, including such diverse places as Texas, Pennsylvania, the Yellowstone, Japan, the Himalayas, and western Europe. Great sheets of ice from the Pleistocene epoch restricted the tree to western North America. "The primordial forests did not fall to timber harvesters, they fell to evolution.

"There are three species extant today; the Coastal Redwood of California and Oregon, the Sierra Redwood in Central California, and the Dawn Redwood in China.

"The two American species, Coastal (sempervirens), and Sierra (gigantia), are both *more* prolific and *more* abundant today than they ever were before the advent of the timber industries.

"*For every tree that is harvested, from five to twelve or more young trees will grow up from the roots of the fallen mature tree.*

"Of all American conifers, the redwood is the most impossible to destroy by logging.

"The myth that these trees take hundreds of years to grow is quickly dashed when one looks at the thousands of acres of fifty and sixty-year old timber stands that have attained the same scenic stature and material size as those of three hundred years past. Simply stated, when the new trees don't have to compete with other plants, (like thickets of brush), and when the young sprouts are not victimized by fires, the redwoods are among the fastest growing, and most prolific trees in America.

"Now listen up:

There are more and better stands of redwood today, by far, than there were before the loggers ever came to the redwood forest! That's not a myth, it's a well known fact among all the loggers in Northern California, and among any real student of natural resources.

"Have you been inundated with the fancy that the redwood forest is disappearing? Well, friend, that's propaganda, pure and simple. There is no possible way to annihilate a redwood forest by logging, and to top that off, the best way to assure the stagnation of a redwood forest is to lock it up. The old timber rots, the unstable trees blow down, and the waste is incredible. *All those redwoods that were clear cut a generation ago are now covered completely with young, healthy, vigorous forests that guarantee a future for our children. That's reality.*

"So the tree sitters explained that saving the old growth is sacrosanct. What they didn't explain is that mother nature will not stand for it.

"It seemed reasonable to the forest industries people to preserve certain areas of old growth, if only for study, and exploration. Therefore, the *owners of timber lands themselves* donated thousands of acres to be set aside for public exploration. Unfortunately, that wasn't good enough. The enviro-freaks wanted it all, and were willing to resort to the most horrendous campaign of propaganda to get their way. Small wonder. That's the way they make their living.

"Now, in northern California, they have only a few political representatives, because there isn't a huge population base. Out of the San Francisco Bay area, and out of L.A., they have a horde of representatives, all vying for public popularity. Naturally, saving Bambi is ever popular, and that's where the votes are. It doesn't make a damn bit of difference what the truth is, if the urbanites in southern California think the forest is being devastated, and that's what they see on the boob tube, then guess which way the votes go?

"You're not talking about a democratic process at all. You're talking about mob rule.

"Let me move on to another voluptuous antic in postulated theory that our eco-freak friends are pompously promulgating:

Environmentalists site overgrazing as the destroyer of western ranges! One of the worst eco-disasters is the conversion of western grasslands into desert by overgrazing! Here vast wastelands of shadscale have taken over where perennial grasses have been wiped out! Cheatgrass deserts now dominate once plentiful ranges that are being devastated by cattle and sheep! Environmental impact statements site the exploitation of rangelands by greedy ranchers for selfish gain as the villain responsible for the annihilation of the west!

"Who will buy the story? Everybody in the urban world will buy it. Why not, if they don't know any better? And how can a Westerner (who's already convicted by the media) ever package reality in saleable form?

"We have millions of acres of excellent, well preserved rangelands that have been in use for generations. But how many people in L.A. or New York can even explain the difference between buck brush and white sage? How many city folks can stand up and tell us the difference between a north Idaho cedar, and a southern Idaho juniper? How many can even tell perennial grasses from annual grasses? Yet, these are the people who rule the west, not us.

"Hell, if I were a city girl, and some TV documentary that was put over by supposed professionals told me that overgrazing was destroying the ranges out west, well, sure I'd believe it. Especially if the film showed me a rangeland that had been utilized. It appears on the tube that we're eating up Bambi's food with our wicked cows and sheep.

"Us ruralites are in such an incredible minority, and we're so damn busy busting our backsides trying to make a living, we have no way to counter the affront. We don't have hundreds of thousands of people sending us money to live on while we spread some zany dogma across the metro plain. We gotta work for a living (unlike our fervent environmental cult friends).

"So here is a presentation for the city dweller," she sighed, hoping that somehow her message would get through.

"Grazing began millions of years ago, spanning countless generations.

"Suppose that a herd of buffalo concentrated in one small area, (as they often do), the forage for that year, in that area, will be consumed, right down to the dirt, but don't fret, it'll be back the next time the rain falls.

"Rangelands often burn, especially so in the case of unused rangeland, and in the space of a few hours, the pristine species and lush forage are reduced to a black void; but, the grasses will be back with the next spring's rain.

"There have been many changes in the rangeland ecology over the past century, and there always will be, regardless of human emotion. The environment is subject to change, even radical change, with or without the illusion of the influence of legislation. It is the command of nature.

"In summer, the grass dries up by nature's decree. That shouldn't be too hard for a metro audience to comprehend. Unused range is more susceptible to fire than range that is grazed. That shouldn't be too hard to understand either.

"The charges that our rangelands are being victimized by desertification is ludicrous, we know that. We have more species of grass than we ever have had, and I'll cite just a few that pop into my mind. Varieties aplenty of rye grass, wheat grass, bunch grass, foxtail, squirreltail, wild clover, fescue, redtop, brome, and dozens of others.

"The basis for excellent range for all grazing animals is the availability of mixed grasses and browse. Mixed grasses fall into two basic groups, namely, annual, and perennial. Since cattle have large, split hooves, and a short, weak hoofstroke, they are physically incapable of pawing up a perennial plant. Horses, however, with solid hooves and long, powerful hoofstrokes, can and do destroy perennials whenever they get short of feed.

"Cattle have short necks, wide muzzles, and *only one row of teeth on the bottom of their muzzles!* The upper muzzle in cattle, sheep, deer, bighorns, and other ruminants *have no teeth at all*, and unless the soils are so extremely delicate that the roots of the plants are easily pulled up, the physical destruction of perennials by ruminant animals is *not*, in my estimation, possible.

"Perennials die when the same plants are interfered with for too many years in a row. If a perennial is overgrazed, that means it was used too hard for too many years in sequence, and never reached maturity. Crucial vitamins and nutrients must be photosynthesized—put into the perennial's root system, and this can only be accomplished by allowing the plant to reach an mature stage of growth once every few years. Rangeland users are one hundred percent aware of this fact, and rotate their livestock as a matter of course, specifically to allow for the need. Their lives depend on the sustained yield of their range.

"Tall wheat is a great basin grass that receded from over use in the early American grazing era, but it's far from gone, and is on it's way to proliferation in well managed areas.

"Crested wheat is an imported species that took root and has been incredibly productive. It is a measure against fire, for it holds moisture longer than most grasses, and its esthetic value is boundless. In cases where livestock, grazing wildlife, insects, fires, or drought hit the same plants for too many years in a row, the perennials recede, and the annuals take over. There is no acceptable theory which demonstrates the inferiority of annuals, and annual grasses (like cheat) are very nutritious. But, when favorable environmental conditions return, perennials will easily reclaim annual stands.

"To give you an example of what the radical calls the devastation of the ranges, let's go to the heart of the wilderness in central Idaho. Here there is a massive granitic (made of granite) intrusion in the surface of the earth (better known as the Sawtooth Mountain and Salmon River Range). This granitic intrusion is called an emerged batholith by geologists.

"What it constitutes is a huge range of granitic ridges and mountains, and the composition of this range is such that the soils are extremely delicate. The reason the soils are delicate is because, in plain talk, 'granite crumbles. It crumbles, because it's made of crumbly rock. Granite.'

"Here is the eco-freak's position:

The mixed grasslands in the central Idaho batholith were devastated by overgrazing! Perennials were utterly destroyed! This is the type of ruthless, capitalistic exploitation that has permeated the western range ecology, and destroyed the natural balance of pristine areas!

"Yes, there are areas that have been overgrazed by livestock. Well, we're perfectly competent to deal with these problems on a state by state basis. There's no need to import a twenty megaton federal bureaucracy to run rough shod over our civil rights, and screw up the management of our range resources.

"The facts are that generations ago, many perennials were 'sheeped off', and receded. To the best of my knowledge, this is true. The question that hits me is, why do they call it devastation?

"Let's go back to a more *'pristine'* era; the era of the emergence of the batholith. When the batholith first emerged, there was a limitation of organic matter, and it is assumed that there was no vascular plant life at all.(Vascular means grass, trees, etc. Non-vascular means moss, lichens, etc.)

"You see, when these mountains first came up, it was all solid rock. Since perennial grasses must collect organic matter to acquire a root system, how did the plants get to the top of the granitic ranges in the first place? Let's think it over.

"Organic matter moves in many ways. Ash, dust, and biodegraded plant life moves in the air, but not to a great degree, unless there's a nearby volcano or some such thing. The prime movers of organic litter in many cases are attributed to grazing animals. The early mammals quite undoubtedly moved organic matter up the slopes, stage by stage, and provided an environment for pioneer grasses. Plant life may well have begun in the primitive area largely because of grazing animals and their deposits of stool. The required elements to sustain a perennial grass stand are: "Mineral soil, air, sunlight, water, and the crucial element here, organic matter. If this environmental condition exists, there will be plant life.

"So, the air, sun, soil, and water was plentiful on these bare, granitic, 'pristine' ranges, but since little or no organic matter was at first extant, there would have been *no vascular plant life at all.* This is an evolutionary supposition.

"Suppose that grazing animals helped bring the organic matter, gradually, from the valley floors up. These animals scattered seed and matter through their stool. Thus, plant life on the granitic ranges was presumable aided by early mammals.

"Now, when plant life flourished, and grazing animals flourished, this was a new era. A new *pristine* era. Remember that word, *pristine.* You will hear it often touted by the environmental cults. It is a somewhat ambiguous term that can be used to describe any new era, even today. Today, like then, there are many pristine eras and areas, to be followed by new, crisp, clean, pristine eras and areas in the future. A new growth of range or forest is pristine by nature, whether the resource was used by man, animal, or consumed by fire, does not matter. New growth is new growth, and that's a pristine condition, either way.

"But grazing animals have always been a part of rangeland ecology, and you can't study the one without the other, because they don't exist apart from each other.

"When man came, massive bands of sheep grazed this pristine area, and in the delicate granitic soils, the perennial root systems that were hewn together with clumps of organic and fragile granitic matter were damaged. Many perennial grasses (it is reported) receded from the ranges.

"Recall the necessary elements for grazing lands; mineral soil, air, water, and organic matter. Did these ingredients disappear? No. Organic matter and the other elements remained in abundance. Annual grasses (pioneer grasses) gather this organic matter from its disintegrated state, and put it together in such a way that there is a bed of organic humus matter once again. The result? The stage is set for a new cycle of perennials. Annuals can be easily uprooted, and when passed through the stool of any grazing animal, whether by deer, elk, horse, cow, or ewe, a strong environment for perennials is made stronger.

"Do you know what the batholith in central Idaho is experiencing today? A perennial phase-in? Correct. Complete with Idaho fescue; tall, intermediate, and western wheat grass; Indian rice grass, and a host of others, as well as an abundance of annual grasses.

"There's your devastation of the wilderness by overgrazing, and this is in the Pacific Northwest's most delicate soils!

"Considering that organic matter is passed by grazing animals, are sheep physically capable of removing organic matter, air, sunlight, mineral soils, water, or any one of these factors from the ranges? No. Hell no.

"Is any grazing animal capable of this feat? No. Hell no.

"Now you answer the crucial question for yourself: Is the devastation of a rangeland by grazing animals a physical possibility?

"Overgrazing can help cause soil erosion, but grazing animals are designed by nature to build and aerate soils, planting seed wherever they go. Before a rangeland could be devastated, the grazing animals, no matter whether it would be cattle, horses, bison, antelope, or whatever, they would all die of starvation long before the range could be devastated.

"When you're talking about massive soil erosion, grazing is only a contributing factor, along with prolonged drought, sequences of fire, insect infestations, torrential rains, and a host of other causes.

"Even in a case where the animals have overgrazed, perennials like sage, shadscale, and other browse plants will immediately spring up, shed their leaves, and start a brand new cycle of annuals.

"Productivity can be aided by reclamation and innovation by individuals who are closely tied to the specific regions. This seems to be the most practical method of restoration when mustangs, wild game, cattle or sheep have overgrazed the land. "But when the environmental cults go howling like rabid coyotes about the devastation of the ranges, well, that's been the most prolific distribution of organic matter in this century. "In short, fires, insects, hailstorms, thunderstorms, drought, torrential rains, as well as grazing, all have an effect on rangeland ecology, but since the stockman's very existence depends upon range conditions, it is highly unlikely that a stockman would set out to 'ruin the range for selfish gain.' There would be no gain for the stockman or anyone else in that. In reality, land users are best served by conservation of natural resources. The sustained yield of the range is the top priority, and has been for generations.

"Since the stockmen have been taking such a pounding, let me show you how ridiculous it really gets." She picked up a local newspaper, and quoted from an article:

"Vast wastelands of shadscale have taken over where lush grasslands were once bountiful! Cheatgrass deserts now dominate once plentiful ranges where overgrazing annihilated the flora and foliage!

"Do you want to know what's funny? This is from a local paper in Mountain Home Idaho, which is an air force town. Most of the people on base are all from out of state. They'd have no idea what shadscale even is. The supposedly 'devastated rangelands' that the writer is recommending for federal protection are so far from water, they've hardly even been grazed, except by migrating wildlife, and the reason there are no lush grasslands, is because the soil is so full of alkaline, it's partially sterile. There never were any lush grasslands with bountiful flora blowing in the wind, except down in the valleys where the soil is so rich they're growing twenty-five ton to the acre of corn!

"And how many people on base know that we are blessed with shadscale, as it's a protein rich shrub plant that makes our country a haven for wintering wildlife as well as cattle? If stripped by the narrow muzzled deer, antelope, and bighorn, it recedes. If pruned, by the wide-muzzled cow, it roots out and flourishes. That's why we have so much of it. Sparse vegetation in areas where shadscale and greasewood dominate are not the result of human exploitation. It's the result of soil, mineral, and weather conditions.

"But how many people in town know that? Hell, you could tell 'em that shadscale is poison, and if nobody told them otherwise, why wouldn't they believe it? They'd never know the difference. Yet, those are the people who call the shots, just because they outnumber us a jillion to one. Well, we better sally on out and educate these good folks, or we're gonna lose our assets.

"Okay. So there's at least nine lawfully identified multiple values of public lands, listed somewhat like this:

1. Recreation
2. Range
3. Timber
4. Minerals
5. Watershed
6. Wildlife
7. Scenic
8. Scientific
9. Historic

"The wilderness cults will argue that their designated areas do not interfere with these other uses of public lands, and claim:

There is no conflict between any of the multiple uses of public domain and wilderness designation. The areas to be designated are remote, inaccessible, roadless, and endangered, greatly in need of federal protection to preserve the pristine quality of the natural environment.

"The envirocults seem to have a great propensity for lying. We've been using all these regions for generations. The way these rascals have got the law rigged up, any road that's maintained only by the passage of a vehicle, is not a legal road, and they can close it, whether we like it or not. In any of these western states, they've got the potential to shut down access to anywhere from fifty percent, to ninety percent of our resource base. It damn sure wipes out all other uses of public lands, and their half baked pretense that if it isn't locked up, it'll be devastated doesn't wash to well with the fact that we've had generations of access to, and generations of use of, all the remaining areas proposed for designated Wilderness.

"The idea that if a wilderness isn't locked up, it isn't a wilderness, well, that doesn't wash with us either, because we're the ones who spent our lives in the wild, and all these Hollywood philanthropers who are trying to tell us what demented souls we have for not seeing things their way haven't got the foggiest notion what the nature of our environment is really like.

"We've had our little four-wheel-drive roads and trails ever since God was a kid, and we've been the ones who kept the country clean, who blazed the trails, who maintained the wildlife populations, and even though we've fought amongst ourselves on various occasions, when it comes to separating fantasy from fact, we're the ones who know the difference.

"Now they come out and marvel at the beauty of our public lands, then go home and tell all the politicians it must be protected! Who the hell do they think has been taking care of it all these years? *Smokey the Bear?*

"There is no point in trying to stereotype the urban public, but, I was talking to a girl from L.A. one day, and I asked her about public land resources. Do you know how the conversation went? Something like this:

"How familiar are you with public lands issues?" I inquired.

"Not very," she replied, "But I just read a book by Hollywood Richard, and it had a lot in there about the way they're cutting down our forests."

Now Hollywood Richard is one of my favorite writers, and the guy is a bona fide genius when it comes to literature. He had three back to back bestsellers, and this one was a great love story. But a lot of the text concerned his personal war with the B.L.M in Oregon over management of forestlands.

"What did you get out of that story?" I asked the girl, curious and apprehensive.

"Well, I think they were selling trees off our parklands." She replied.

"Did you know there is a difference between parklands and public lands in general?"

"No," she stated timidly, "It just said that they were cutting down all the trees."

"Well," I explained to her patiently, "Roughly one third of the continent is public domain, did you know that?"

She didn't.

"And," I went on, "Hollywood Richard was not referring to parklands in his book. He was referring to public lands in general. Did you know that Oregon is being hit by one of the worst infestations of pinebeetles in the nation? Did you know that the forests up there are dying by the tens of thousands of acres, and if the forest resources aren't harvested, they're going to go up in smoke?"

She didn't know that either. All she knew was that Hollywood Richard told her they were cutting down all the trees.

"Did you know that in most western regions the vast percentage of all resources come off public lands, and that forest harvest in parklands is never allowed? *Did you know that if our access to public lands continues to be cut off we're going to have fires out here that will make the '88 Yellowstone burn look like a weiner roast?*"

I hate to be redundant, but she didn't know that either.

"What do you think would happen to all the people in the western states if the harvest of resources on public lands were not allowed?"

"I don't know," she admitted blandly, "I've never really thought about it, but I mean, like fires and stuff, aren't they kind of natural?"

"Wouldn't it be natural if the city of L.A. burned to the ground, and all the flowers and birds had homes again?"

"Well, gee, that's different," she surmised, "I mean there's a lot of people there, you know?"

"So, what you mean is, the people in the cities, they count, and the people in the mountains, they don't count at all, right?"

"Well, no, that isn't what I mean......I just never thought about it that way."

"Oh," I replied sagely, "Well did you ever stop to think about where all your material goods come from?"

"Well, we could like, import it, you know what I mean?"

"Do you think that importing raw materials will stop our national forests and rangelands from going up in smoke?"

"Well, no, but I mean, what happens when all the trees are gone? When all the loggers have cut them down, then what will we do?"

"Are you aware that in Oregon they have some of the fastest growing timber stands on earth? Are you aware that the loggers replant more forests than they actually harvest?"

She shook her pretty head.

"Are you aware that they don't even stop at locking up the public lands, that they come right in and condemn the private lands as well?"

Same response.

"Are you aware that they have already locked up over one hundred million acres of national forest land, just in designated Wilderness areas alone, *not even counting the national parks, wild and scenic rivers, state parks, wildlife refuges, bird sanctuaries, and so forth?*"

Nope.

"Are you aware of the havoc that was wrought in the wake of the mustang protection bill? Are you aware that five hundred residential properties were flattened and hauled off in Ohio to make a national park? Are you aware that the bureaucracies have a strangle hold on all the western economies?"

Nope.

"Are you aware of the difference between socialism and capitalism?"

Sorry. She wasn't.

"Can you tell me the difference between a north Idaho cedar and a southern Idaho juniper?"

No way.

"Could you recognized the difference between a grazing band of mustangs and a grazing band of range horse?"

She didn't know there was a difference. All she knew was that somebody was eating up all the range, and cutting down all the trees.

"Are you aware that there are more redwoods today than there have been in the last two hundred years?"

Nix.

"Do you know the difference between a California bighorn and a Rocky Mountain Bighorn? Are you aware that most of the waterholes that desert big game animals use were built by stockmen? Are you aware that there is a consolidated effort among all the environmental groups to wipe out foresting and ranching on public lands entirely? Are you aware that the western states cannot survive without the use of public lands?"

She didn't, and she wasn't.

"Are you aware that there is a bill before the congress in Washington D.C. that would appropriate one billion dollars per year to be used to wipe out private property rights, and add millions of more acres to the public lands network, when they already own over a third of the country?"

She'd never heard of it.

"Do you even give a damn at all?"

"Well, I, ummm, I never thought about it before."

"But when you go to vote for a politician, you'll vote for the one who says he's going to save the forest, and the mustangs, and protect nature from the wicked, evil land users, right?"

"Well, I would, probably...or at least, before I listened to you I would have."

"Hasn't anybody ever told you any of these things before?"

"No."

"Maybe this girl was not a prototype of the average urban mind, but the conversation was real, and the ignorance of actual circumstances out here is all too prevalent.

"And so you see, the enemy is within us. We have failed to communicate. There was nothing wrong with that girl. She wasn't a socialist, or a capitalist, or a parasite, or a crusaded. All she knew was what she'd been programmed to believe, *and to change all that, we're gonna have to start talking, demonstrating, boycotting, lobbying, and bombarding the metro audiences with accurate information, or we might as well pack up our bags, go to L.A. and get on welfare.*

"We're going to have to sell state's rights and regional control to the downtown crowds, or else start applying for jobs in the bureaucracies. The people in the cities don't understand, and if we fail to make them understand, we're going to lose it all. It's really that simple. *Communicate, and fight for state's rights, or go broke, and join the enemy.*

"Are you ready for the cultist's great *eco-compromise?* Here's the way it works:

The only way to solve these dilemmas on public lands is to compromise. It seems only reasonable and rational that the lands users should be willing to bargain from a compromising position, because, after all, it is federal land, and the owners are the people of the nation. Therefore, a reasonable agreement in land management practices must be bargained for on that basis. We have proposed another one hundred and fifty million acres to be designated wilderness, but we're willing to settle for less than half that amount. What could be more reasonable?

"Let me tell you, folks, the city people will eat that up. It sounds real pretty. What the cults aren't telling them is that we've already compromised ourselves right out of our homes.

"Initially they came in with a proposal for a million or so acres in Idaho, and were willing to settle for much less. When they had the Frank Church Wilderness locked up, they came in with a new proposal. You guessed it, another million or so, and they were willing to settle for much less. Eventually, they got a half a million more acres of our best country. Now they had all of the original million that they were willing to settle for half of, and here they came again. They only wanted two million more, and were willing to compromise for less than half of that *reasonable* amount. They compromised their way right into four million acres, and now they're ready to compromise, half of what they want, every time they make a new proposal. You guessed it again. They want nine million more acres of B.L.M. just in Idaho!

"We start compromising with these monkeys, and that means they get it all, and we get screwed, only, in a very compromising way. They already have over a hundred million national acres on ice, just in designated wilderness, and proposed wilderness. Throw in umpteen million acres of national parks, God knows how many million acres of state parks, untold hundreds of miles of protected wild river drainages, several hundred thousand acres of wild horse refuges, add in all the reserves and preserves for birds, big game, old growth, spotted owls, birds of prey, and couple all that with the one billion dollars per year they want to use to take over private land and convert it to public land—are you ready to compromise?

Sounds reasonable, right guys?

Let's progress toward a mutual compromise. Why should we be stubborn? That would be bad for our public image!

"Let's have a little compromise in Oregon over the spotted owl controversy. The birdie boys figure that Oregon should sacrifice twenty-five hundred acres of old growth timber *per pair* of spotted owl! Pretty cheeky deal, huh? If they can come in with half that amount, they just wiped out several billion dollars per year from Oregon's timber economy, which naturally drains the industry further, which naturally weakens their ability to fight the enviro-cults on the wilderness front, the parks front, the land acquisition front, and every other front.

They're attacking from so many fronts, the Westerners don't even know where the battleground is!

"Well, I'll tell you where it is. It's right between the ears of those metropolitan audiences, *and don't you ever forget it!*

"Here's a little bulletin on the spotted owl that Ranger Rick won't tell you about. The spotted owl issue is just a smokescreen for the taking of more land. *These hardy little creatures will nest in second growth, and third growth, and they do it all the time.* The birdie boys will tell you that if a few million acres of old growth is not set aside, the birdies will go bye-bye. Well, every study done on these little birdies contradicts what the public lands panderers are telling you, and the birds contradict it themselves. They nest and thrive in young timber stands all the damn time—but you won't hear *that* in the birdie-boys' report to congress—wanna bet?

"The objective is to beat down the industry's resistance to the socialization of the west. Are you listening, downtown America? Well, it'd be a good idea to open up your ears, because believe me brethren, *you're next!!*

"Anytime an invading political doctrine can take over the strength of a nation, which is it's resource base, then they've got the rest of the country by the proverbial testes. Don't believe me? Just stay your present course, and it's *adios amigo*. You're history.

"*Paranoia!* The eco-cults will rail!

"Paranoia, my posterior! Look at the stats! They already own and control over a third of the land mass of the nation, and they have plans to rip off a billion dollars per year in tax dollars, just to smilingly acquire millions of acres more! Our noble intentions toward our environment have been gloriously prostituted with our own tax dollars!

"Now, I can't stop this political monster by myself. It's going to take the most powerful political consolidation the west has ever known. We have a choice between democracy, and bureaucracy. We don't have time to moan and wring our hands. We need action, and we need it *now!*

"Look at some of the absurd charges that have sent the land users running for their holes:

Cattle grazing farmlands are ruining habitat for game birds! Overgrazing is responsible for big game starvation in winter! Watersheds are being animated! Strip mining is wiping out the mountains!

"Now how in the hell could all that be happening when they've already locked up over half of the public lands, have plans to take over the rest of it, and condemn millions of acres more for the panderer's playground? The fact is, it doesn't matter what the facts are. They're ready, willing, and able to argue that *their* facts are true, and *ours* are lies. They'll argue that water is land and land is water, if they can get a law pounded through congress. And as long as it's mob rule, instead of regional control, they'll compromise their way into the take over of every rural community in America. You say it can't happen here? Well, it's an ongoing program, and it's been happening in ever increasing increments for years.

"*The environmental issues are just smokescreens for the takeover.* That became painfully obvious many years ago. Now, we've got the chore of undoing what we already let them do. They brainwashed the public, now our job is to unbrainwash them, and the only way we're gonna do that is to convince the metro crowds that we can handle the environmental problems without surrendering our lives to socialist authoritarianism.

"We've got to show the city folks that they are losing their rights on public lands right along with us, and that if they'll grant us the sovereignty to manage public lands on a state by state level, it will not only *get the looters out of their pockets,* it will also establish better control and management of our public lands, and a cleaner, healthier, environment.

"If we let that billion dollar per year acquisition become law, we're going to have a god-almighty political war on our hands that will make our former lost battles look tiny. And while we're barely getting consolidated to fight on a domestic level, these turkeys are putting the finishing touches on the most beautifully orchestrated piece of federalism that America has ever known.

"I see no alternative to pooling our resouces on an innerstate basis if we plan on overcoming the odds. The time has come to face the reality that confronts us, and deal with it objectively. Our views of environmental issues must be communicated clearly, and effectively, packaged and sold to the metropolitan audiences on a massive scale. It is not just our land that is at stake, it is their land as well, and they have a perfect right to know what the truth is.

****

"Okay," she continued, going back to the simple explanations that she hoped would find their way to the cities, "let me tell you a few interesting things about big game starvation in winter that is laid at the door of the cattlemen, just to give you a few new ideas.

"Cattle are primarily grass animals with a low percentage of browse in their diet. Big game animals are grazers also, of course, but by and large they are browsers, with a lesser amount of grass in their diet. In a harsh winter, the crucial staple for big game is browse, and, as previously mentioned, cattle, unless severely confined, not only serve to enhance the growth of browse, they are physically incapable of stripping or uprooting it.

"Grasses in severe winters are *covered with snow*. The snow crusts, and big game would get sore feet and sore noses from rooting for grass until the temperatures rise, so they concentrate on browse. Thick, old forests have a bitter impact on the availability of browse, for the dead timber and thick stands choke it out, and, when the snow sets in, the deadfall timber becomes a death trap for wintering herds, because in these areas, they have no mobility in the snow. Predatory animals would feast on them if they used those areas, and their instinct tells them to *steer clear*. They migrate to the open plains, fields, and basins in the lower elevations.

"The wild accusations against our farmers and ranchers are worse than dangerous. They condemn our farmland and take it away, when the farmers themselves have been providing habitat for millions of species of wildlife and waterfowl by growing grain crops and hay crops in the millions of tons!

"I was watching *Hollywood Marty's wilderness* program on public TV. They showed all the little animals—a raccoon, a deer, a coyote, and various others—then they showed the wicked, evil farmer who was destroying the habitat by growing corn. Don't the city people realize that every one of those animals thrive on corn and other grain crops? Don't they consider that land users grow hay by the millions of tons, and feed tens of thousands of big game animals every winter? Hell, no, the city people don't realize it, because dear Marty forgot to tell them that part!

"Do they realize that a designated wilderness area violates their civil rights by denying access into our best recreational areas? Do they even know we've had access into all these regions for generations? Do they realize that closing all our roads on public lands means that the elderly, the handicapped, and little children are obliged to hike for miles on end just to get to the Saturday morning fishing hole? Don't they realize that without resources from public lands the west is dead? Did dear Marty and dear Richard stop to think that this is the most bigotted and discriminating lock up in American history? Do the metro audiences even take a minute to think about it? Do any of the Hollywooders even think about it before they do those commercials? Do any of these people ever stop and wonder if they're being manipulated by leaders of a political front that might have some serious ulterior motives that have nothing to do with environmental issues at all?

"I doubt it. I doubt that it even crosses their minds.

"Well, it's no big news story to us. We've been aware of it for years, and totally helpless to stop it. There's never been a consolidated movement from the west to do anything but concede.

"We ran out of money long before we ran out of guts, and our dearest hope was that we could negotiate an agreeable, and *final, compromise.*

"But what did we get?

"A hundred and fifty million more acres of designated Wilderness proposed, a ten million acre expansion plan for the National Parks, a billion dollar per year tax rip to impiement unlimited federal land acquisition, grazing fees hike proposals, across the board road closures, twenty-five hundred acres per pair of spotted owls to be set aside, off road vehicle taxes, fees and fines, twice as many personnel in the bureaucracies, a lawsuit that the Sierra Club filed in Colorado to win water rights all the way down an entire river drainage, scores of millions per year for the feral horsies, forest fires that wiped out our resource bases, land set aside proposals galore for the grizzly bears, (as if the bears will be able to read the signs that tell them where they're supposed to be), the condemnation of private property all along the western coast for birdie sanctuaries (as if the birdies aren't there already), a multitude of other proposals too long to list in one book, and to cap it all off, the crowning jewel of the envirocult's invasion:

THE GREY WOLF REINTRODUCTION PLAN!!

She tried not to laugh, but it was impossible. Of all the dogmas that the ecocults had sold to the urban public, that had to be the *coup d gras.*

"Well, so much for compromise. *You talk about land acquisition!* If we don't start surrendering millions of acres for our friendly neighborhood wolfies, we're going to be

condemned as dogmatic, biased, unsophisticated barbarians who just are so terrified of wolfies, because our mommies read us the story of *Little Red Riding Hood.*
"You think I'm making a joke? *I ain't!!* The proponents of the wolf plan are telling people that we have a socially conditioned bias against wolves, because when we were little kids, the stories we heard about the big, bad, wolf caused us to tremble in fear! No joke! *That's what they're saying!!*
"Come to Idaho, and check it out! After the outright theft of four million acres, just for Wilderness, a thirty mile stretch of the Snake River for birds of prey (soon to be expanded to a sixty mile stretch), a cavalcade of locked-up resources on hundreds of miles of Wild Rivers, Parks, reserves and preserves until they're running out our ears, nine million acres more of Wilderness study areas, *and now:*

THEY PLAN TO THROW IN A ONE POINT ONE MILLION ACRE WOLF RESERVE!!! JUST FOR STARTERS!!!

"And if we don't like it, well, we're just biased, and don't like the wolfies, because our mommies read us all those scary stories.

HOLY JUMPED UP MOTHER OF BAMBI!! WHAT IN THE SAM BILLY HELL WILL THEY THINK OF NEXT??!!

"Sorry, gang. I ain't buying the compromise routine. It won't work. The eco-freaks are going to force us into the most awesome political battle of this century, and it's a battle we can't afford to lose. *If we lose, it's soviet city out here, and that's the bottom line.*

"A designated wilderness area, worse than any other form of socialization of public land, undermines our fragile economy by bureaucratic expansion, counterproductive government activity, and the theft of all our wealth.

"The most tragic result of the entire wilderness fiasco is the *exploitation of human ignorance to serve the narcissistic dogmas of a select few*. Propaganda and demagoguery are used to create a *false illusion* of the public opinion on which the demagogue thrives. The illusion of virtue has gone unquestioned by the might of a *supposed* majority, which in reality *does not exist!* Is this the environmental cultist's objective? Well, sure it is, and worse than that.

"People in the cities are not stupid, or wicked, or anything else. They're just normal people, like you and me. They are savvy enough to realize that our own species is as important and as integral a part of the world ecosystem as any other species, and indeed it is every man's responsibility to care about the environment. They quite simply have no idea what in the hell is going on out here!

"We must appeal to human integrity, and intelligence, leaving coercion and propaganda to the demagogues. Beware the death trap set by ignorance and coercion. This is the only world we have.

****

"No matter how many times I examine the ramifications that go hand in hand with the wilderness dogma, I return to the question of the legitimacy of the bill per se.

"The social implications alone should be enough to rescind it entirely, or at least modify its form, and restructure its content to allow for reasonable access.

"I hope to have outlined a basic format, and laid a foundation for a premise on which to begin a new, victorious battle with this ridiculous piece of legislation.

"There's nothing wrong with keeping wild lands wild, rivers clean, game populations healthy, and tourist enchanted with our spectacular public lands.

"But there is something wrong with the socialization of private property, the authoritarian practices of the federal bureaucracies, the seizing of the nation's wealth, and the prostitution of conscientious environmental goals.

"I hope to have provoked more thought on the issue of designated Wilderness, and the incredible spectrum of collectivism that goes with it. It should be made plain to our urban neighbors that if *we* fall to the hands of socialism, so do *they*, eventually.

"There is nothing about the socialist dogma that is beneficial to our environment, and there are no environmental issues in the western states that cannot be handled competently be the elected officials within the states themselves.

"As far as the need to provide healthy homes for mustangs, big game, fish, and all wild animals, yes, even including some carefully controlled numbers of wolfies in a few isolated areas, the western people are very sympathetic with the urban plea.

"It is not because of some mythical innate hatred, or socially conditioned bias against the wilderness and wild animals that we have come to despise the federal bureaucracies, and have undertaken the task of promoting state's rights and regional control.

It is quite simply a matter of survival.

"It is not my intention to direct malice toward anyone, or to mislead my audience. It is purely from the standpoint of civil rights that I have put forth this presentation, and I wished to point out a few things about the federally designated Wilderness areas that the urban populations may be generally unaware of.

"Perhaps the American Congress would like to rewrite the English language, so that there would be no interpreting their dialog. Think. The average man is not as foolish as the administrators would force him to be. The dictionary defines a road as:

1. A long stretch of smooth or paved surface made for passage by vehicle, carriage, etc.

2. A way, or course.

"When one of our bountiful wilderness areas is federally designated, the roads are closed, because the Wilderness stipulations read that any road that is maintained only by the passage of vehicles is not a *legal* road, and shall be closed, which denies access entirely, except for backpackers and horsemen. In many of the western states the vast percentage of the land will qualify for a *Wilderness Study Area,* which is locked-up just the same as if it were *Designated Wilderness.*

"Now for show, the envirocults will televise an oldster or two, hiking through the wilderness, and will even go so far as to import some willing handicapped, and assist them into the back country, but it's like a white bigot with a token black in his administration. The mainstream of physically limited people are locked out completely. It is also far too expensive for the normal person to take a wilderness vacation in a designated area. How many people can afford a pack trip, or a month off from work to really get back into the mountains? The weekend sportsman is also out of luck, and one hundred million acres is overdoing it somewhat, let alone the proposed one hundred and fifty million more.

"There is no lack of understanding of environmental issues by the people who oppose the Wilderness designations, but rather, a difference of opinion. Every road, way, and trail in these areas serves a specific purpose. These roads, ways, and trails have been maintained for generations by constant use. They lead to private property, cow camps, logging camps, mining claims; many are for sportsmen's access, firefighting access, firewood and polecutting access, and the roads and trails to and through the natural divisions in the topography are there for specific reasons. The nature of our environment discourages aimless wandering in vehicles, and the lands included in all the remaining proposed areas are in reality not roadless at all. Many millions of acres that we had use of and access to for generations have already been taken away. There were and are many roads, and the road closures will have to be carried out *by force*.

"Suppose that a grandson is three years old, and a grandfather is seventy years old. Grandpa wants to take the lad fishing, back to the places where his grandpa used to take him when he was a child. He relates to these areas spiritually, as well as mentally, and physically, because out there, he first discovered the wonder of the wilderness. He wants to pass that spiritual experience on to his grandson. But, because grandpa is too old to hike or go horseback for miles, and because grandson is too young, these two people are cast out of all our best wilderness areas that should, by all that is morally right, be open to them. The same is true with the handicapped person.

"If this fact alone does not constitute discrimination, then there is no such thing as discrimination, and it really doesn't matter what the legally defined terms of wilderness designation have been rigged to compensate for, it does not alter the radical nature of this terrible injustice.

"There is no benefit to metropolitan America in this type of bigotted ploy. There is no benefit to Mother Earth in separating man from nature. *How in God's name can anyone perpetrate an act as despicable as that, and call himself a friend of the earth?*

"Common sense should tell us not to clear cut a forest of Douglas Fir in an arid, soil poor area that will not likely come back. You don't need federal legislation to figure that out.

"Certain other areas, when clear cuts are made, come back exceptionally well, and that mode is instrumental to reforestation, depending on environmental conditions, like insects, fire hazards, etc. You don't need the fed to help you figure that out, either.

"There is no need to mine an exceptionally scenic area, and that also is a matter of common sense.

"There is a fortune to be made in freelance reclamation for the entrepreneur with the drive and desire to get the job done, and it shouldn't take federal legislation to force the issue. Why not put the millions of dollars that are squandered on socializing the land to the practical use of reclaiming some of the land that has been used too hard?

"The conservation of natural resources can and does have a beneficial impact, and it is vital that people work together to solve their existential needs, but the chore needn't involve the point of a gun.

****

"I have nothing against the idea of an eastern student or a girl from the city coming out west to take up an active role in public land management, but I would like to stress the vulnerability of that young person's mind. It seems rather bizarre that a youngster can come to the west, and in a few short years, become such a master of the wilderness that he or she can politically overpower an entire region.

"It also seems rather bizarre that a little club representing a tiny minority can recruit some of the most wealthy sponsors in the world. Or, could it be the other way around—that the youngsters were recruited by the sponsors?

"At any rate, it is no less bizarre that our entire western culture could be so easily induced to hang its head, and give up the fight for truth.

"We spend millions upon millions in our colleges and universities out here. What kinds of trails have our children been travelling that they cannot have a more significant effect on the management of natural resources?

"There are some incredibly intelligent students from the east, from the west, from all over the world. Why is it, then, that an environmental movement to do something besides wage political wars cannot be constructed? Why is it that this kind of intellectual strength cannot be directed towards reclamation, rather than dogmatic incantation?

****

"You buy them books, and you send them to school, and what the hell do they do? They eat the covers.

****

71

"In summing up, I would like to take the time to dismiss the notion that the Wilderness issue is a matter of right or left wing politics.It is most definitely a bi-partisan concern. I hope that the views I have outlined here will not be rubber-stamped 'Right Wing,' because nothing could be further from the truth. Regardness what particular camp of social philosophy a person comes from, it should be readily admitted that *bureaucracy does not work*. More Wilderness set asides mean more bureaucracy, and our entire nation has been drowning in the stuff for too many years. *Democracy* does not mean *socialism*, any more than *Republic* means *a military state*.

"And so, to help my friends out there understand the nature of this thing, I will offer a set of ideas that might throw a new light on the problem. Everywhere I turn, people are asking:

'Why are they locking up our wilderness?' Is it some sort of socialistic conspiracy?

"I think not. A conspiracy is supposed to be a covert activity, and this thing is much too flagrant for that. The far left is there, ringing all their collectivist bells, but it's no conspiracy, it's just a dogma that the city people have fallen for, hook, line, and sinker, without every understanding the flip side, or taken a glance at what's coming through the back door. The socialist front is just seizing an opportunity to exploit a convenient situation.

'Is it the work of a handful of elite demons?'

"I think not. It's just a fraud that was well packaged and well promoted.

'Is it simply an irrational lashing out of social anger because of the way the eastern states fell to the onslaught of the machine age?'

"Well, perhaps in part, but let me explain to you how I have come to look at this thing, and how I try to rationalize the cause.

"There is a symbolic-symbiotic relationship between Man and Earth, not unlike the relationship between mother and child, in the respect that Man sprang out from Earth, and relates to her as the *mother of life*." She paused, collecting her thoughts.

"Man is born from her, and he roams her vastness in search of existential and spiritual needs. Drawing from the resources available, he survives as a quasi-adaptive species. While changing physically, mentally, and spiritually to adapt to the changing environment, he also learns to modify the environment to fit his particular needs.

"As his social and spiritual character evolve, so do the desires of his soul. As his reason and intellect develop, corresponding to his loss of physiological adaptability, his basic hunter-food gatherer instincts are weakened—many are lost.

"Man has become a creature who, more and more, modifies the environment in order to survive as a species that is less and less instinctive.

"The biophilic orientation, that is, the character structure based on Man's identifying with the natural world, is superceded by a cybernetic orientation, an orientation based on his identifying with a world of machines.

73

"Cybernetic Man has become so alienated from the biological world that he perceives his experiences in the wilderness as sacred escapades into paradise—a paradise that he sometimes believes has shunned him.

"The symbiotic tie to Mother Earth is still tugging at the core of his soul, calling him, and at the same time rejecting him, haunting him with the certainty that the Garden of Eden was real, and he has been cast out from it by the actions of generations past; for the Garden of Eden is not unlike the anthropological theory of that time in prehistory when primitive man lived peacefully, in a world of relative abundance.

"The craving to return to the former evolutionary era, the Garden of Eden, buried in the bosom of Mother Earth, is correspondent to Cybernetic Man's dilemma. Thrust into a world of machines, with a nuclear death cloud hanging over his head, his fear of being born into an automated world beyond his comprehension causes this mental dysfunction.

"It is the biophilic orientation, rooted to the core of his being, that begs him escape from social reality, and the frightening responsibilities it bears. Thus the need for this sacred experience, the wilderness experience, is vital to his identity, and, quite probably, his very survival.

"Man's struggle to balance reason with instinct includes a struggle to gain a new identity—a compromise between his cybernetic identity, and his biophilic identity. His spiritual evolution dictates his moral credence, and the drive to live according to his moral conscience is putting him on a higher and higher spiritual plane. Maintaining the standards of this new plane of consciousness draws him to this high calling—to make himself worthy of his ideals. The more time he spends on this mental plateau, the more his reason supercedes his instinct.

"Man must transcend the cybernetic dilemma, if he is to retain his identity. He must face the world he is born into, solve his existential and spiritual problems, while revering the sanctity of the earth. Respecting the needs of the natural world, he can achieve this new identity, and he will no longer be a castaway, but an integral part of a much greater world.

"This, then, is the reason I find for the desperate struggle for control of public lands. The identity that the hunter finds in the search for wild game. The identity that the naturalist finds in oneness with the earth. The identity that the logger finds in the mastering of his science; that the Indian finds in spiritual communion with his ancestors; that the grandparent finds in sharing the wilderness with his progeny.

"Most crucially, I feel it should be the backbone of our social identity, and that this enlightening association with nature can be readily obtained in every region of the earth, by the inhabitants of those regions.

"But consider the total ineptitude of bureaucratic control. Consider the way that millions upon millions of acres of our best country has been locked up by the federal government in complying with the popular whims of the environmental cults. The social damage already done by bureaucratism and socialism in government is staggering. So why should we trust our wilderness to them?

"Yes, the pristine qualities of our West can and will be preserved, as they have been for generations. But there is no need for a twenty megaton bureaucracy to run rough shod over our civil rights.

They are not saving our wilderness, they are locking it up.

"In most cases, as with the mustang situation, the solutions to the concerns of the urban world are simple and basic. National coalitions of concerned people can do an immense amount of good if their efforts are directed appropriately.

A simple resolution to keep the natural balance should certainly replace the current dogmas that prevail. Keep it simple. It really is not such a complexity, when viewed from the correct philosophical premise.

"Surely most of the things I have published herein are things that have been thought of before, but I know that a fair judgement has not arrived. It seems that the dominant judgement will be the one with the most money behind it, and I cannot see the fairness in that, especially with the way the fed is doling out the dollars to the socialist machine.

"It also seems that our western intellectuals cannot get over the philosophical hump that the public lands issue presents without getting into a ridiculous harangue between socialism and capitalism. Well, how about another story for our intellectual friends:

"There was once a tree with hundreds of bird nests. The birds all shared the tree, which was an entity unto itself. The tree was, to the birds, a collective property, but the nests in the tree were private property, and they were defended with the lives of the individual birds. The birds had common sense in the matter.

"Our western intellectuals, it seems, have descended so low that even the birds seem to be wiser, and can better distinguish the idea that collective properties and private properties are both products of nature, and that the one does not do anything but compliment the other.

"It is interesting and alarming to think that we may only be seeing the tip of the iceberg. Since our radical friends have discovered that they can railroad us at will from the cities (by swaying the metro vote with grossly inaccurate and very well publicized misinformation making us out to be idiots); does it not follow that they will continue to do so at will? I see no movement from the West that is powerful enough to stop them.

Perhaps we are in dire need of a giant coalition from the West. If we don't have one, we may certainly lose it all.

"Think about what has happened to us to date. Then think that it is surely only the beginning. I think about that. I think about it often, and I urge the recall of the wilderness bill for revision and further study, as the full scope of this thing has not been clearly identified.

76

"I question the entire premise of the wilderness dogma, because of the suspicion that it is based on the idea that Man is an enemy to nature.

"If it is not based on that format, then why the forced separation of Man from nature?

"In closing, I submit that the social and spiritual aspects of man's relationship to nature should be clearly defined, and accepted as a major role in the multiple use concept of public land management, and that state's rights is the practical solution that the metropolitan residents of America can readily identify with, and should certainly concede to without any further delay."

****

The firelight blazed orange and turned white as it reflected off her perfect form. She stood poised, like a listening doe. Her ivory skin held an aura from the light illuminated by the pitch black that the night thrust against it. Her silky hair lay softly over the nipples of her breasts, and her arms were outstretched—her fingertips holding the darkness.

Outside the cabin there was silence in the valley of the long grass. The wind had stilled, and the skies had parted.

There was a break into the clouds as though reason's crystal rapier had parted the storm to let her prayer slip away into heaven.

In the cabin, the firelight dimmed. She turned off the recorder and pulled a blanket over her shoulders as she lay down on the rug. The coals popped in the purring fireplace as the starlight that had shone outside died silently.

With a rush, the winds were upon the cabin again, and the voices of her ancestors howled through the canyons and the rugged mountains of the Idaho wilderness. Hail pounded down until it nearly shook the ground, and raging storm clouds sent blackness into deeper oblivion.

When she arose, there was a flood of red-gold light from the tips of the Sawtooth Range, and she rushed outside where the sparkling morning air caressed her skin, then she smiled.

It was the promise of an Idaho morning—the kind of perfect blue that only Idaho can know, and the kind of perfect land that only God can make. The wind that whispered in the rimrock without touching the ground was a silent assurance to her soul, and she waited for the words that she knew the land would whisper as the sun began a crimson blaze over the mountains.

Then the land said the words that meant so much more than a thousand books could ever say, and the words meant the truth to the way her spirit rose and revelled in the things we all hold sacred—out here. They settled through the air from the wings of an eagle that rose on the heights of the morning air to greet the dawning, and she heard them as clearly as if they had been spoken by God:

"Ee Da How."